Towards a New Bretton Woods

Challenges for the World Financial and Trading System

Report by a Commonwealth Study Group

Commonwealth Secretariat
Marlborough House, Pall Mall, London SW1.

Published by
The Commonwealth Secretariat
Marlborough House
Pall Mall
London SW1Y 5HX

Distributed by
Longman Group Limited
Fourth Avenue
Harlow
Essex CM19 5AA

ISBN 0 582 90261 4

Price £5.00

Foreword by the Commonwealth Secretary-General

At their annual meeting in September 1982, on the eve of that year's meeting of the International Monetary Fund and World Bank, Finance Ministers of the Commonwealth, who represent one third of the world's nations, noted the vast politico-economic changes which have taken place since the establishment of the Bretton Woods institutions and called for a study of the global financial and trading system as a whole and the role of the international economic institutions.

Developments since then have confirmed the value of an examination of this kind. Bretton Woods was a landmark event in post-war history in which the international community responded to the need to fashion a financial and monetary system to avert the kind of economic disaster that had engulfed the world in the 1930s. The intellectual creativity of White and Keynes was matched by a vigorous spirit of internationalism in setting in place an innovative institutional framework to help the world economy make sturdy progress.

Bretton Woods created the International Monetary Fund (IMF) to preside over a world of relatively stable exchange rates and with the capacity to assist countries when they faced temporary difficulties in their balance of payments. It also set up the World Bank which, having assisted reconstruction in war-damaged Europe, provided finance for development in newly emergent Third World countries. These two institutions, together with the General Agreement on Tariffs and Trade (GATT) which helped to liberalise trade in manufactures, were part of a system which helped the world economy to advance up to the 1960s. World output rose steadily, and world trade even faster, bringing higher incomes and improved standards of living worldwide.

The seventies changed all that, and the position has become worse in this decade. The 1971 United States suspension of the convertibility of dollars to gold, on which the monetary system was pivoted, marked the collapse of that system, later confirmed by the 1976 Jamaica agreement on floating exchange rates. The first oil price rise, in 1973, was a further shock, creating unprecedented surpluses and equally huge deficits. Commercial banks stepped in smartly to recycle the surpluses; this helped to sustain the world economy in the early years of recession. But, as the recession continued, world trade ceased to expand, trade barriers increased, output fell and export earnings dropped. Growth was stunted and unemployment rose to record levels. Exchange rates became increasingly volatile, while high inflation and high interest rates held back investment and raised the cost of repaying debts. Countries which had borrowed large sums from the banks approached economic collapse and leading banks themselves faced the prospect of default by borrowers.

A major banking crisis has been averted, with emergency packages put together for several countries on the brink of insolvency. But the danger of a banking collapse, through default by a large borrower, remains and the adjustments forced on debt-burdened countries are further depressing the world economy as it struggles to lift itself.

Some signs of recovery have now appeared in the US and to a more limited degree in a few other Western industrial countries, but there is no certainty that recovery will be vigorous or durable. Inflation has been brought down but interest rates remain high, particularly in the United States, and the gyrations in exchange rates continue.

It is in this context of prolonged and severe malfunctioning of the world financial and trading system that the demand for reform of the system and the principal institutions which serve it has gathered strength. While the call for reform was earlier made principally by developing countries, most of which had not emerged as nations at the time of Bretton Woods and so could not influence its outcome, the manifest disarray and dangers of the last few years and the increased evidence of interdependence between North and South and between growth, trade and finance have greatly enlarged the constituency that seeks a review of the system as a whole.

In the past year, there has been intensive discussion in many forums of the state of the world economy. At the level of Heads of Government, there have been the Non-Aligned Summit in New Delhi and the summit of industrial countries at Williamsburg. There have been ministerial-level meetings of the GATT, the Group of 77 and of OECD, the Interim and Development Committees of the IMF/World Bank, and most recently UNCTAD in Belgrade. Additionally, there have been meetings of other inter-governmental bodies and expert consultations. At the end of it all, however, there remains widespread and gathering unease over the capacity of the international community, with its

iv

present institutions and arrangements, to restore the world economy to a course of stable progress.

Despite signs of recovery in some industrial countries, the developing world faces continuing, if not worsening, hardship on all fronts. If recovery falters or is feeble, most developing countries will be forced to make further severe adjustments, which could only result in greater impoverishment of their people. Even a substantial general improvement in the world economy may not by itself prevent further deprivation in many poor countries. Financial liquidity is not all that is at stake; in many countries, political stability too will be at risk.

Finance Ministers, in calling for this study, pointed out that while the Bretton Woods framework had evolved to an extent with changes in world economic circumstances, it had failed to keep abreast of these changes. The vast scale of today's capital movements, of disequilibria in external payments, of foreign debt, and of the operations of multinational companies, as well as the extent of global interdependence, could hardly have been envisaged at the time of Bretton Woods.

The economic changes that have taken place are not merely quantitative in nature, though in that respect they are formidable enough. They are qualitative individually, and even more so collectively. Production, trade and financial flows have all become much more international; the interdependence of countries, and interaction between economic transactions in different fields, have also increased. Protectionism has effects, for instance, not just on trade and therefore on growth but also on the capacity to repay debts and consequently on the health of the banking system. The nature of these changes and the new relationships they signal underscore the need for a fresh look at the financial and trading system as a whole. Reform of the framework of finance and trade and the role of the main institutions has today become indispensable if we are to strengthen our capacity to manage the world economy and set it on a more orderly path.

The study is the work of a distinguished group of experts, bringing together specialised knowledge and experience at the highest level in the fields of reserve and commercial banking, investment finance and international economic policy, under the chairmanship of Professor Gerry Helleiner of the University of Toronto. It is the first comprehensive study of these issues to be made on a North-South basis under inter-governmental auspices. It addresses both immediate concerns and long-term issues both of substance and of process. While it specifically disclaims the intention of prescribing individual national policies, the group points out that its mandate relates to the international aspects of those policies and adds that international rules and institutions can ultimately function only if governments allow them to.

In the course of its work, the group was assisted by a number of people with specialised knowledge on the functioning of the international economic system who willingly agreed to share their expertise, in many cases in the form of papers. A selection of these contributions is being published separately by the Commonwealth Secretariat.

The study represents a consensus within a group eminently well placed both to understand the implications of the present situation for national and international progress and to assess the technical feasibility of its proposals. Although much can be done to meet the most urgent problems within the existing international framework, the study concludes that the time is ripe for a process of reform and renewal to reinforce and broaden recovery and hence lead to sustained growth in both developed and developing countries as well as to promote a more efficient, stable and equitable international economic system.

I am confident that the study will be seen as a significant contribution to the conceptual and practical preparation for a fresh attempt to design a world financial and trading framework that responds to the world's current needs and mankind's aspirations for stable progress. In answering a Commonwealth call, it offers service to a wider world.

SHRIDATH S. RAMPHAL

Letter of Presentation

Marlborough House,
London, SW1.

27 July 1983

H.E. Mr. S.S. Ramphal,
Commonwealth Secretary-General,
Marlborough House,
Pall Mall,
London, SW1.

Dear Secretary-General,

We are grateful for your trust and confidence in appointing us to serve as a Commonwealth Study Group to examine the international financial and trading system, in accordance with a request by Commonwealth Finance Ministers at their Meeting in London in August 1982.

We enclose our Report which represents the unanimous conclusions of the Group. As an independent Group, we sign the Report in our personal capacities, and not as representatives of governments, institutions or countries.

We wish to acknowledge the invaluable advice and assistance we received during the course of our work from a number of persons and institutions, including members of the governing boards and senior staffs of the World Bank, IMF, UNCTAD and the GATT. We are also grateful to a number of experts who helped by writing papers for us.

We have benefited enormously from the excellent supportive arrangements provided throughout by the staff of the Commonwealth Secretariat.

Your personal encouragement, at the outset, and your continuing interest in our work have been much appreciated.

Yours sincerely,

G.K. Helleiner

Conrad Blyth

K.K.S. Dadzie

William Demas

Stuart Harris

Lal Jayawardena

Jeremy Morse

Harry M. Osha

I.G. Patel

Contents

Chapter

Chapter

Appendix

Chapter 1

Introduction

1.1 When the Ministers of Finance of the Commonwealth asked in August 1982 for an overall examination of the international trade and payments system, the economic scene was very dark. On top of the difficulties caused by worldwide recession and inflation, protection was increasing and a debt crisis was imminent in a number of countries. There are now signs of some improvement in the international situation. Vigorous action by both debtors and creditors has eased the debt crisis for the time being; and there is some economic recovery in the industrialised countries. But the goal of sustained non-inflationary growth is far from being achieved, and in the meantime the costs of very large and sudden adjustments in many countries have yet to be revealed.

1.2 Behind these immediate problems lie longer-term questions with which the Ministers were concerned. While they accepted that 'the institutional framework had evolved to an extent with changes in world circumstances, such evolution had not kept pace with developments'. They considered that 'in view of the vast politico-economic changes which had taken place since the establishment of the Bretton Woods institutions, there was an urgent need for a new overall examination of the international trade and payments system as a whole and in particular the role of the international economic institutions'.[1]

1.3 Many questions are raised in any such fundamental review of the international economic system. How well has the Bretton Woods

---

1. Communiqué of Commonwealth Finance Ministers, London, August 1982. For the purposes of this Report, the Bretton Woods institutions have been taken to be the General Agreement on Tariffs and Trade (GATT) as well as the International Monetary Fund (IMF) and the World Bank Group.

system worked? Has it adapted sufficiently to the changes in the world economy that have taken place since the 1944 Bretton Woods Conference? Can instability be reduced? Can adjustment processes be improved? Can more orderly patterns of liquidity provision and financial flows be established? Are the arrangements for trade and finance sufficiently co-ordinated? These and other issues have been borne in mind in the preparation of this Report. But to put them into some sort of perspective, the remainder of this chapter sets out a few brief details on the recent developments in the world economy and the underlying objectives on which its financial and trading system has been based.

State of the World Economy

1.4   The recent performance of the world economy has evidently been unsatisfactory. The 1970s were characterised by severe instabilities and weaknesses in economic performance. Growth rates in most countries fell sharply and unemployment and inflation rates rose. Two major oil price shocks aggravated other difficulties and contributed to major structural imbalances in international payments.

1.5   During 1980-82 the world suffered the longest and most pervasive recession since the Second World War. Total real output in the industrialised countries stagnated, production of manufactures in many of them fell to the levels of 1976-77, and capacity was consequently severely underutilised. Unemployment in these countries, particularly severe among the young, reached the highest levels since the Second World War, implying very large losses of potential output and income. Even in severe recession real interest rates have been far higher than historical norms. The collapse of fixed investment has limited productivity improvement, implying slower long-run growth and quite possibly contributing to immediate inflationary pressure. Until lately, inflation continued at rapid rates; despite recent declines in its pace in the major industrialised countries, there is no assurance that recovery will not bring the return of higher rates.

1.6   The volume of world trade ceased to grow in 1981 and actually declined by 2 per cent in 1982. Imports by the industrialised countries have been falling since 1980. Uncertainties and international divergencies both in official policies and in rates of inflation have contributed to volatility and apparent misalignments of major currencies' exchange rates. Slower growth and the stagnation of world trade, as well as uncertainty, have increased the pressures for protection.

1.7   The effects of the recession and its associated problems upon the non-oil-exporting developing countries have been severe. Countries exporting primary products have experienced particularly sharp deterioration in their terms of trade. Middle-income exporters of manufactured products have also been severely hit by stagnant demand and protectionism in their major markets. Growth rates have consequently fallen — in most cases implying stagnant or declining per capita income — and overt urban unemployment, already high, has risen.

1.8 Deteriorating trade performance and high interest rates have together created enormous debt-servicing problems for many developing countries. Medium- and long-term external debt of the non-OPEC developing countries now totals over $500 billion,[1] and there are substantial further amounts of short-term commercial debt. Since the third quarter of 1982 commercial bank lending to these countries has been severely cut back — adding further to the squeeze on them. A large number of developing countries are now in arrears on commercial bank debt. Emergency rescheduling of external debt and tough domestic austerity programmes have kept the international financial system functioning but anxiety persists as to its fundamental health. The required adjustment programmes pose in many cases a serious threat to the political stability of the indebted developing countries as well as to their resumption of growth in the near future.

Fundamental Objectives

1.9 An overall examination of the international trade and payments system, such as we have been asked to undertake, requires criteria against which to judge the efficacy of the system as a whole and of the institutions within it. In most countries the principal objectives of economic policy are taken as: growth of real income per head, full employment, price stability, equitable distribution of income and wealth, and a reasonable degree of national independence. Conflicts among these objectives are inevitable and all countries accept 'trade-offs' among them as they develop policies that aim at the attainment of the objectives as a whole.

1.10 At the international level, and in the context of the pursuit of world peace and stability, including stability in the economic sphere, similar objectives have been expressed from time to time. They were expressed, with remarkable consistency, in the articles of agreement of the Bretton Woods institutions as well as in the unratified charter of the International Trade Organization recommended by the 1947-48 Havana Conference (see Appendix I). While there may at times have been

---

1. All references to dollars in this Report are to United States dollars.

differences of emphasis, to which there will be reference in this Report, we do not believe that the overall aims and objectives specified by the international community at the time it established the framework of the present international system have changed significantly. It is those that underlie this Report. They reflected then and reflect now a common acceptance of broad objectives such as:

— the encouragement of overall growth of global output, employment and international trade and exchange;

— the promotion of efficiency in the use of resources, national and international;

— the avoidance of price inflation;

— the reduction of instability and uncertainty in the movement of prices, output, incomes and employment;

— the promotion of appropriate adjustment to economic shocks and changes at the global and national levels; and

— the achievement of equity in the sharing of benefits and opportunities in the international economy.

1.11 While purely national policies are obviously of crucial importance for achieving these objectives, appropriate international policies have always been seen as critical to their achievement as well. The international financial and trading system which was seen then, as now, to be essential to these objectives was a system which was universal, and based on a number of fundamental principles, notably, multilateralism, non-discrimination, and openness or transparency. More generally, for its membership of predominantly market-based economies, the system aimed at limiting governmental intervention in international trade and exchange, thereby reducing the scope for international conflict and, by liberalising trade and exchange, encouraging greater international co-operation in other areas. It also sought to govern international economic relationships by a system of rules rather than by discretionary management by those with economic or political power. Underlying those principles and agreed approaches were a number of additional assumptions, the most important of which was that national governments would pursue policies to achieve full employment and domestic stability.

1.12 On one matter of principle and approach, it is best to be explicit at the outset. Non-discrimination does not imply uniformity of treatment. We accept the case, already recognised in parts of the international system, for special treatment for the poorer countries, most of which were not yet independent at the time of Bretton Woods. Particularly in hard times such as the world is going through now, it is the poorer countries which generally suffer the most. What is more, from the long-term perspective, the growth of even the poorest economies can contribute to the growth of the world economy. For widely accepted humane and political reasons, no less than for economic ones, the system has to continue to take account of their special needs.

1.13 A related issue is that of appropriate power-sharing in international economic institutions. In the context of growing interdependence and the need to evolve a more co-operative international system, continuing progress in power-sharing is an important objective. A concomitant of interdependence is shared management. Beyond noting its importance, we have not directed our attention to this issue in our Report.

Perspective of the Report

1.14 Despite some successes in post-war international economic co-operation, there have evidently been major failures. Important changes have also taken place — giving rise to new problems, and unease as to systemic capacities to deal with them. Among the suggestions that have been put forward within the past year to improve the global economic prospect is that for 'another Bretton Woods'.

1.15 We have not interpreted the call for 'another Bretton Woods' as simply a call for another conference. A premature and ill-prepared conference could easily be counter-productive. Rather, we have interpreted it as a call for renewed work towards agreed international objectives, such as those set out above, in the same spirit of optimism and creativity and with the same awareness of the costs of non-co-operation as were shown at the Bretton Woods and Havana conferences nearly forty years ago. The precise mechanisms for pursuing such efforts should themselves be matters for discussion; the principal criterion for assessing the means of proceeding, which may at some point include a major international conference, must be what may prove most effective. We have therefore devoted the bulk of our effort to sorting out the issues rather than elaborating the potential role of a conference.

1.16 We share the hope that the spirit of Bretton Woods can today be recaptured without the need for the prior global trauma which so influenced the participants on that occasion. We are convinced that the world need not continue to lurch from crisis to crisis, to fear another deep depression, or to abandon the aspirations for a more liberal and equitable world economy.

1.17 Even if a healthy global recovery soon materialises, suffering and political tensions are bound to remain high for some time to come.

There are underlying difficulties in the global economy which recovery in itself will not correct. We therefore see the present moment as propitious for sustained effort toward longer-run reform. At the same time, just as long-run systemic failures contributed to the present problems, so failure to handle short-run problems appropriately may generate grave problems for the longer-run objectives.

1.18 In Chapter 2, to establish the context for what follows, we review the most important changes in the world economy since Bretton Woods, particularly those of the last ten years. In Chapter 3 we deal with the immediate economic situation, and begin to consider ways of making the international system more stable in future. This examination continues in Chapter 4 in which we discuss international liquidity and the role of the IMF. Chapter 5 discusses commercial bank finance and the more effective management of debt problems. In Chapter 6 we consider longer-term finance for development, suggesting a pattern of financial flows which is less reliant on commercial banks, and emphasising the roles of equity finance, the multilateral development banks, and official development assistance. In Chapter 7 we deal with trade arrangements and the role of the GATT, with particular attention to their linkage with the financial system. Chapter 8 considers contingency arrangements against the possibility that sustained non-inflationary recovery may not be forthcoming. In Chapter 9 we suggest the next steps which might be taken, offering possible procedures for international discussion of improvements to the financial and trading system. Finally, in Chapter 10 we summarise the Report and draw together our recommendations for action in the immediate future, in the near-future and in the longer-term.

Chapter 2

Evolution of the International Economic System

Rationale and Purposes

2.1 The bitter experience of the 1930s and the Second World War demonstrated the need for increased international co-operation in money, finance and trade. Before reviewing the changes which have taken place since the creation of the IMF, the World Bank and the GATT in the 1940s, it is important to consider briefly the rationale and purposes of the financial and trading system of which these three bodies were the pillars.

2.2 The IMF's principal mandate was the improvement of international monetary arrangements. In the inter-war period, exchange restrictions and competitive devaluations had been widely employed in pursuit of trade and employment objectives; and, inevitably, resort to the use of such national policy instruments led to retaliatory measures on the part of trading partners. At the same time, inadequate international liquidity had contributed substantially to the economic difficulties of the 1930s. While the IMF provided 'machinery for consultation and collaboration on international monetary problems', it sought, through its par value system, to promote greater exchange rate order and stability, and, by the provision of temporary finance, to discourage resort to 'measures destructive of national or international prosperity' (e.g. inappropriate resort to deflation and devaluation or protection) in response to payments imbalances. Its role with respect to trade and the attainment of overall objectives of economic policy was explicit: 'to facilitate the expansion and balanced growth of international trade, and to contribute thereby to the promotion and maintenance of high levels of employment and real income and to the development of the productive resources of all members as primary objectives of economic policy'.[1]

2.3   The rules established for goods trade under the GATT, though much less ambitious than those of the proposed International Trade Organization,[1] were designed to promote the objective of a multilateral, non-discriminatory and transparent trading system. To do so, all protective measures except tariffs were prohibited, with exemptions only for special cases. A liberal approach to trade was to be sought through multilateral negotiations conducted on the basis of overall reciprocity. Non-discrimination was to be achieved through the requirement of unconditional most favoured nation (mfn) treatment, wherein 'any advantage, favour, privilege or immunity granted by any contracting party to any other country... shall be accorded immediately and unconditionally to... all other contracting parties'. In effect, tariff concessions were to be negotiated bilaterally between major parties on the basis of reciprocity but then extended to others on an unconditional mfn basis.

2.4   The World Bank was originally designed in large part to encourage private investment and, when that was not available on reasonable terms, to provide its own longer-term credit for the reconstruction of war-ravaged economies or for development of underdeveloped countries (thus its formal name: International Bank for Reconstruction and Development). It was to intermediate between nervous private lenders and capital-hungry sovereign borrowers in circumstances where international bond markets had virtually ceased to function.

2.5   At the time that these monetary, financial and trading arrangements were framed, it was assumed that: (i) national policies would effectively preserve the objective of full employment, thus reducing pressures on international instruments; (ii) the global economy was predominantly a private market-based system, although attempts were made to accommodate centrally planned economies; and (iii) following the inter-war experience and the post-war disruptive circumstances, private investment and credit would be of relatively small importance. Although not a large element in thinking at the time, a further implicit presumption was the need for concessional finance in various forms to supplement developmental credit provided both to war-affected economies and the developing countries.

---

1.   The formal purposes for which the three Bretton Woods institutions were set up are given in Appendix I, which also gives the objectives of the still-born International Trade Organization.

2.6   The major elements of the international system thus reflected an understanding that the private market system would need the supplement of some form of international management or, at least, some understandings on rules and procedures, to promote the efficient use of real resources on a worldwide basis. The establishment of an efficient financial and trading system was seen as the supplying of a 'collective good'. There was, in addition, a recognition that even efficient markets may not distribute their benefits equitably and that some redistribution was likely to be necessary. Despite the many changes in the international economy since Bretton Woods, these understandings and approaches remain basically valid. They constitute the rationale - today as then - for continued effort to construct a universal multilateral and open international economic system such as that originally envisaged at Bretton Woods.

Adaptation and Change in the System

2.7   The creation of the Bretton Woods institutions represented a bold attempt to promote multilateralism in a universal system with clear rules in which nations could expect fair treatment in economic affairs regardless of political affiliations. The institutions made important contributions to post-war reconstruction and to the remarkable period of sustained growth of world production and trade in the 1950s and 1960s. Despite gaps and areas of weakness and a tendency to buckle when put under too much stress, they encouraged a level of international co-operation far in advance of anything achieved in the pre-war period.

2.8   In the monetary field, a fairly stable system of exchange rates was maintained up to the early 1970s. The capacity of the IMF to provide liquidity increased, though it still remained small; liquidity continued to be based mainly on the dollar. At the World Bank, resources expanded and, with the establishment of the International Development Association and the International Finance Corporation, new directions and forms of support were introduced. In trade policy, GATT's existence solidified national commitments to the principle of liberal and non-discriminatory international trade and considerable progress was made in reducing tariff barriers on manufactures. Built-in economic stabilisers in the domestic management of the industrialised countries were introduced; they reduced the dimensions of economic shocks transmitted between nations and the risks of cumulative downward spirals of the kind experienced in the 1930s. Many new international institutions were established in the search for increased international co-operation and stabilisation. All these developments promoted a degree of stability and harmony in the international economy.

2.9   International economic events have a momentum of their own, however, going beyond the activities of these post-war international institutions, important though they certainly are. Nearly forty years have now passed since the Bretton Woods institutions were created. Consideration of the capacities of these and other existing international institutions to deal adequately with the economic problems of the rest of the twentieth century and beyond requires that stock be taken of the changes in the overall international system since they were established and the adequacy of their adaptations to those changes.

2.10 Some of the changes are long-run and may be of a permanent character. Others, however, are the product of more recent international events. Among the major changes and issues which deserve attention, the following stand-out:

— increasing international interdependence;

— increased governmental participation and involvement in national market economies, not least via the continuing growth of military and defence expenditures;

— the much larger number of countries and the expanding role of the developing countries in the world economy;

— the growing, though still uncertain, place of the centrally planned economies;

— increased uncertainty over the possibility of combining full employment with non-inflationary growth;

— new dimensions to problems of balance-of-payments adjustment;

— the growth of bank finance relative to official financing;

— floating exchange rates;

— the emergence of the multiple currency reserve system;

— a deteriorating environment for world trade;

— a new salience for energy issues, notably pricing and security of supply; and

— declining support for internationalism and multilateralism.

Each of these changes is commented upon in the following sections.

Increasing international interdependence

2.11 Over the past thirty or so years the whole concept of international relations has changed. While interdependence is not a new phenomenon, today, more than every before, no nation state is wholly independent — whether economically, militarily, politically, environmentally, socially or culturally. Whilst the 'shrinkage' of the globe has been the product primarily of the great developments in international transport and telecommunications, it has also been the result of conscious economic policy. The decline in tariffs on trade in manufactures during the quarter century to the mid-1970s, together with the widespread liberalisation of exchange controls beginning in the late 1950s, was associated with dramatic and sustained expansion in international trade, finance and real investment. World trade grew over this period at a rate around twice that of world production, and world production grew at unprecedented rates. A major force in the growth of international trade was transnational corporations engaging increasingly in 'international production'. Expanded international labour flows were also an important feature of the prosperous post-war period.

2.12 While increased international interdependence offered benefits, it also brought new problems. Individual national economies are now more vulnerable to developments in other parts of the world economy. The potential for almost instantaneous movements of capital across borders has diminished the capacity of individual governments to manage their exchange rates or control the course of domestic monetary events, and thus has created new macro-economic management difficulties. The growth of interdependence also led to increased synchronisation of business cycles and, in consequence, eventually to some increase in their intensity at the global level. Among those experiencing increased vulnerability in this sense are many developing countries that have only relatively recently 'opened' themselves to international exchange.

2.13 Post-war growth in the industrialised countries other than the United States resulted in a multipolar world, more difficult to manage and yet, because of increasing integration, requiring either more centralised management or more co-ordination and consistency between decentralised decision-makers. Some improvements in management arrangements have slowly been emerging. Among the industrialised countries, the creation of such new institutional arrangements as the OECD, the Group of Ten (G10) and the Western Economic Summits, were steps towards the kind of co-operation demanded by emerging political and economic developments. Unfortunately, these may also represent the narrowing of global mananagement arrangements to a relatively small group of major countries. Efforts at expanded regional and South-South economic co-operation have also been undertaken. Progress at a more universal level has, however, been limited.

2.14 Despite the evident increase in the importance of the international dimensions of macro-economic problems, solutions continued to be pursued almost wholly through independent national policies. Increased interdependence in various forms is a theme which pervades this Report. The implications for improved international policy consultation and co-ordination, to which we attach central importance, are addressed in Chapter 3, and those for other aspects of the global economic system are considered in each of the subsequent chapters.

Increased governmental role in national market economies

2.15 The economic philosophy behind the post-war international economic arrangements was a combination of confidence in the market for resource allocation, as reflected in the liberal aspirations of the GATT, and reliance upon governments, backed by the IMF, for stabilisation and, in particular, the maintenance of full employment. Along with responsibility for employment, governments of industrialised countries gradually accepted expanded responsibilities for other elements of basic welfare, e.g. health care, education, housing, the environment, etc. and, through the resulting public expenditures and the tax system, for the distribution of national income. Developments since 1945 have changed the balance in a number of ways. As explained in later sections of this chapter, the large number of developing countries which have achieved independence has affected the international weight of market forces generally, as has the emerging role of the centrally planned economies.

2.16 Contrary to the underlying presumptions of the GATT, governments also took on ever greater roles in resource allocation. The support of particular sectors such as agriculture had long been seen as a governmental responsibility which unfortunately involved protection. Increasingly, governments also became involved in the support of depressed industries and regions; this support typically was also associated with protective measures. Soon they were also engaged in the active stimulation of potential future industrial 'winners' as well. A further cause of expanding governmental expenditures was the increasing commitment to military and defence objectives. The 'cold war' and the Korean War brought a sharp end to post-war hopes for permanently reduced allocations to these ultimately unproductive purposes. Were the present global expenditures on armaments reallocated to productive investments, it cannot be doubted that employment, output and growth in the world as a whole would be higher. Many of these expanded governmental activities not only increased the size of government expenditures but also reduced their short-term flexibility.

2.17 With the relative decline in the role of the unfettered private market place, in industry, trade and in domestic monetary affairs, more and more domestic governmental policies were likely to generate implications for others outside national borders. Recent efforts in a number of countries to reduce the share of the public sector, and to encourage market forces nationally if not internationally, have not yet significantly changed the total picture. These issues are considered principally in connection with macro-economic management in Chapter 3, and with trade matters in Chapter 7.

The larger number of countries and the role of the developing countries

2.18 When the IMF and the World Bank were established the number of signatories was in the forties, while there were only 23 original contracting parties to the GATT. Political independence still lay ahead of a large number of colonies and protectorates in the less developed areas. At the same time United States leadership in global economic affairs was unquestioned. By the beginning of the 1980s the United States' share of global output had fallen to 22 per cent — from 40 per cent in 1955 — and the world economy had acquired a multipolar character. There were over 140 members of the IMF and the World Bank, and almost 90 contracting parties to the GATT. Many of these countries had different economic systems from the original members, normally with governments playing much larger roles. The diffusion of power and the increase in the number of countries added greatly to the complexity of power-sharing and decision-making arrangements in international economic institutions. The new membership also began to shift the overall consensus as to what these institutions should be doing — towards greater concern for the problems of developing countries.

2.19 In any real sense, developing countries were only marginally involved in the creation and early evolution of the Bretton Woods institutions. In the last three decades, apart from the Third World's growing political voice and rapid growth in numbers, many developing countries have been growing faster than the industrialised countries in economic terms. In the 1970s, joint action by oil-exporting developing countries greatly enlarged their role in the international economic system; and the so-called newly industrialising countries (NICs) became major competitive exporters of manufactured products and important borrowers in world money markets. Developing countries accounted for an estimated 30 per cent of total growth in world output during this decade.

2.20 While increased manufactured exports and substantial borrowing by developing countries led to new frictions and uncertainties in the international economy, they also helped to sustain exports from industrialised countries in a period of slow global growth. In trade in manufactures, developing countries import about four times the value of their exports, a situation which makes their development of major interest to industrialised countries. The developing countries, including the oil-exporters, took over a quarter of the total exports of industrialised countries in 1981. Even excluding the oil-exporters, they constitute a larger market for West European manufactured exports than North America and Japan combined. Similarly, they are more important in this respect to North America than is Japan or Western Europe. A measure of their importance can be gauged by the fact that the drop in imports by the non-oil developing countries accounted for 37 per cent of the fall in world imports in 1982. The industrialised countries cannot achieve a strong sustained recovery unless the developing countries also revive.

2.21 Of the OPEC countries' cumulative investible surpluses of some $370 billion during 1974-81, 80 per cent was invested in industrialised countries, including the commercial banking system which recycled substantial amounts to other countries; 15 per cent of the surplus was made available directly to developing countries as grants and loans. In addition, some OPEC countries, particularly Saudi Arabia, provided substantial resources to the Bretton Woods financial institutions, via loans for the oil and supplementary financing facilities of the IMF and direct purchases of World Bank bonds.

2.22 The developing countries, taken together, are also now major actors in global issues, not only in trade and finance but also in the environment, the oceans, and space. These countries have not so far played a role in global affairs commensurate with their relative stake in the world economy. A system which is truly universal and effective however would require that they share both power and responsibility. The increased role of the developing countries in international economic affairs figures prominently in virtually all the chapters to follow. Chapters 5 and 6 emphasise the important distinction between the middle-income developing countries, which have access to commercial bank finance and foreign private direct investment, and the poorer countries, which are more dependent on aid.

The growing place of the centrally planned economies

2.23 Provision was made in the post-war institutional arrangements for the centrally planned economies. Some of these joined GATT and the IMF, though several of them subsequently withdrew. However, their situation was ambiguous in a system geared primarily to the market.

2.24 Over the last decade or so, the centrally planned economies have become linked much more with the market economies in ways which have considerable significance. The size of East-West trade is already important — for example, during 1979-81, East European countries obtained a third of their imports from the industrialised countries (although this trade made up only 5 per cent of the industrialised countries' exports). So is its character. Apart from the difficulties of reconciling state-trading pricing mechanisms with market pricing, mechanisms such as counter trade, which essentially bilateralise trade with investors from market economies, have become increasingly important in a number of products. Security issues have also been of continuing importance to trade, particularly in strategic commodities, as in the differences over gas sales from the USSR to Western Europe. In addition, several East European countries have borrowed heavily from commercial banks and other financial sources. Their total debt is of the order of $100 billion. This led to severe debt servicing problems in 1981, spreading from Poland to a number of other countries.

2.25 An important aspect of the centrally planned economies' recently increased outward orientation has been renewed interest in their participating in the IMF and the GATT. As many of the rights and obligations in these institutions, notably the recommended liberal trade and exchange regimes, are, on the face of it, primarily applicable to market-oriented economies, membership of the centrally planned economies, including such countries as China and Vietnam, continues to pose special problems. There may also be difficulties with regard to the supply of verifiable economic information. The problems to which these countries' practices give rise and the prospective solutions are of potentially wide relevance since state-trading is common in developing and some industrialised countries. For the centrally planned economies, however, the added political element may make agreements more difficult.

2.26 This Report does not deal at length with the issues surrounding the participation of the centrally planned economies in the international economic system. Its concern with universality and multilateralism requires, however, that they be carefully considered at each stage of any proposed institutional reform, and notably during the process suggested in Chapter 9. The fact that these countries' recent experience has broadly paralleled the ups and downs of the rest of the world may offer some grounds for optimism concerning perceptions of a mutual interest in their full participation in future international economic arrangements.

Uncertainty over the possibility of combining full employment with non-inflationary growth

2.27 The international consensus concerning the full employment objective, reflected in the planning of the post-war international economic institutions, was a major influence in domestic policies of the industrialised countries. In the first two decades after the Second World War a high degree of success was achieved in this area. For the later years of the 1960s and more especially in the 1970s and early 1980s, however, growing inflation, together with evident rigidities in economic structures and systems for wage determination, led to considerable debate about how far inflation and full employment were linked. More particularly, doubts developed as to how successful the industrialised countries were likely to be in future attempts to achieve both full employment and stable prices. Equally, it was expected that growth would take place at lower rates than in the golden post-war decades.

2.28 The inflationary experience of the 1970s had a profound impact upon macro-economic decision-making, and bred severe 'disinflationary' policy responses in the major industrialised countries. In the absence of alternative effective anti-inflationary policies, monetary restraint played a major part in these responses, with possible detrimental effects for longer-run growth. It is still unclear whether inflationary expectations have really been turned around, with the result that policy-makers may continue to incline toward caution as they seek to encourage further recovery and increased employment.

2.29 Even if it involves, at least for some time, a retreat from other desirable objectives such as full employment, the need for non-inflationary growth is now generally accepted. Without lower inflation, whatever the other implications, an effective, equitable and sustainable international economic system is likely to be significantly more difficult to achieve. This Report is concerned, in the first instance, and particularly in Chapter 3, with the restoration of sustained non-inflationary growth, although it is recognised that this may only be achieved at modest rates relative to those of the 1950s and 1960s. The possible implications of failure to achieve it soon are addressed in Chapter 8.

New dimensions to problems of balance-of-payments adjustment

2.30 During the 1970s and early 1980s the still inadequate international arrangements for liquidity came under severe strain as unprecendented demands for balance-of-payments financing emerged. Some attribute the new dimensions of balance-of-payments maladjustments to the high rates of price inflation during this period. Whatever their fundamental causes, the oil price 'shocks' of 1973-74 and 1979-80, and the deep recessions of 1974-75 and 1980-82, required longer-term finance and longer forward commitments than the IMF had previously provided. IMF credit had previously been offered only for relatively short periods, usually three to five years, and advance commitments were not typically provided for more than a year ahead. (Even in the 1950s and 1960s IMF lending had frequently been criticised for its short-term character and its consequently inevitable conditioning on demand management.)

16

2.31 Major relative price changes, such as those of oil prices (and previously, for many developing countries, world food prices), necessitate structural adjustments if they are non-reversible, and longer-term and increased temporary financing whether or not they are eventually reversed. Structural adjustments involving supply-side reallocations require many years to complete. Changes in the relative price of oil, even if reversed somewhat over time, have lasted long enough to contribute importantly to major ongoing balance-of-payments difficulties for oil-importing developing countries, and corresponding adjustment issues for the oil-exporters and the industrialised countries. In addition, the last two worldwide recessions have been of unusual length and severity — in part because of inadequate international mechanisms to support smooth adjustment to major relative price 'shocks' or to ensure some degree of international consistency in anti-inflationary policy. These recessions have generated further terms of trade 'shocks' and consequent need for balance-of-payments adjustments. The unprecedented conjuncture of very high real interest rates with deep recession created particularly severe financing problems for some of the oil-importing developing countries.

2.32 Many oil-importing countries, both industrialised and developing, thus experienced massive current account deficits in both 1974-75 and 1980-81. Although the industrialised countries as a group were able to reduce their deficits within reasonably short periods, there were marked differences in the policies and experiences of individual countries, differences which generated further problems for the international economy. Insufficiently offset elsewhere in the system, deflationary policies generated a marked reduction in global economic activity during both adjustment periods. Yet these policies did not entirely break inflationary expectations. It appears also that the burden of deflationary adjustment in the industrialised countries was borne primarily by investment activity, thus exacerbating underlying structural problems.

2.33 Multilateral financial institutions responded to some extent to the new needs of developing countries — for longer-term and expanded balance-of-payments finance — with changes in some of their previous practices. The IMF created a special 'Oil Facility' after the first oil 'shock', an innovation which was not, however, reintroduced after the second one. It also extended the duration of its lending by introducing an Extended Fund Facility in 1974 which provided for three year credit programmes and repayment over periods now as long as ten years. The World Bank in 1979 introduced a new Structural Adjustment Lending Facility which provided medium- to long-term credit in support of multi-year programmes emphasising supply-side reallocations and improved efficiency. The vast bulk of the new requirements for balance-of-payments finance was, however, met from previously little used and unexpected sources, notably the commercial banks. These issues are considered at greater length in Chapter 4, which deals with the provision of international liquidity, and in Chapter 5, which concerns commercial bank finance and debt.

The growth of bank finance relative to official financing

2.34 During the last ten years increased proportions of international capital flows were channelled through the private banking system. In particular, the role of the international commercial banks in meeting the financial needs of the developing countries grew significantly, as official liquidity expansion, development assistance and private direct investment failed to keep pace. In the wake of the first oil price 'shock' in 1973-74 the banks played an active part in recycling the OPEC surplus and they have continued to channel flows of funds between OPEC, the industrialised countries and the non-oil developing countries. Until very recently, their role in providing short- and medium-term balance-of-payments finance to developing countries dwarfed that of the IMF, except for countries they did not consider creditworthy. Commercial bank credit of this type was generally offered without conditions such as the IMF typically imposes.

2.35 According to the OECD, the total outstanding medium- and long-term debt of non-OPEC developing countries rose from $75 billion in 1971 to $520 billion at the end of 1982. During this time the share of private creditors in that total rose from 49 per cent to 64 per cent. Although some richer developing countries had access to international bond markets, most have had to rely more heavily on syndicated bank credit. Over a third of total medium- and long-term debt outstanding at the end of 1982 was owed to the commercial banks — over a half if publicly-guaranteed export credits are included. Commercial bank lending has been heavily concentrated, however, on four countries — Mexico, Brazil, Argentina and South Korea — which together accounted for about two-thirds of the gross debt of non-OPEC developing countries to commercial banks in the BIS reporting area at the end of 1982. The poorest countries, considered uncreditworthy by commercial lenders, did not borrow significant amounts from the banks.

2.36 The implications of the growth of bank finance and commercial debt are addressed primarily in Chapter 5 but they also figure in the discussions on international liquidity in Chapter 4, on long-term finance in Chapter 6 and on contingency planning in Chapter 8.

Floating exchange rates

2.37 After several crises and a major rescue effort late in 1971, the fixed exchange rate parity (or the adjustable peg) system was finally abandoned early in 1973. At that time most of the major currencies began to float against each other, albeit with some continued central bank management. Although the desirability of 'stable but adjustable par values' was agreed within the IMF's Committee of Twenty, reporting in 1974, the Second Amendment of the IMF Articles in 1976 permitted each member to maintain exchange rate arrangements of its own choice, thereby authorising continued floating. The majority of developing countries continued to peg their currencies to major reserve currencies or, increasingly, to the SDR or other currency 'baskets' of their own choice.[1]

2.38 Floating currencies remained, to a significant extent, managed by national monetary authorities seeking to impart increased stability to their financial and trading systems. To reduce the prospect of mutually incompatible governmental interventions in foreign exchange markets, guidelines on floating were agreed by the IMF Executive Board in 1974. In the Second Amendment these guidelines were replaced by new IMF exchange rate surveillance procedures, but these have not, in fact, proved very influential. Managed exchange rate floating has undoubtedly facilitated balance-of-payments adjustment by providing an increased degree of flexibility in unsettled conditions. But it has also brought unforeseen problems.

2.39 While it was generally expected that the system of floating rates would lead to an increase in the variability of nominal exchange rates, it was not expected that these would be as volatile as they have been. Swings of up to 30 per cent over relatively short periods have become frequent for major currencies. Moreover, interest-responsive and speculative capital flows have led to exchange rates remaining out of line with the requirements of basic balance in international payments, as indicated by competitiveness and other longer-term factors, for periods of 12-18 months or more. This persistent 'over-shooting' and misalignment may involve severe costs — for example, wrong signals and uncertainties for investment decisions, and the aggravation of trade frictions and protectionism. Western Economic Summit conferences have recently devoted considerable attention, and directed further research, to these problems. Here they are addressed in connection with the discussion of stabilisation objectives in Chapter 3.

---

1.   The Special Drawing Right (SDR) is an international reserve asset established by the IMF in 1969 and currently valued in terms of a 'basket' of the currencies of the five major industrialised countries. SDRs are allocated from time to time, as a supplement to other reserves, to IMF members in accordance with their quotas. Members may use SDRs under specified conditions in a variety of transactions, including those to meet balance-of-payments needs. It is also increasingly used as a unit of account and as a peg to fix the value of national currencies.

The emergence of the multiple currency reserve system

2.40 The dollar, originally convertible into gold at a fixed price, was the principal reserve asset held by official monetary authorities and the principal form in which they expanded those reserves over the 1950s and 1960s. According to the IMF, official foreign exchange reserves, most of which were in dollars, increased from SDR 45 billion in 1970 to SDR 102 billion in 1973 and SDR 297 billion in 1980. Despite highly uneven distribution, this explosive growth and the increase in the gold price provided a major rationale for resistance to significant further SDR allocations. Even with the later decline in foreign exchange reserves, at the end of 1982 the SDR component was only 5 per cent of non-gold reserves and a mere 2 per cent of total reserves (including gold valued at market prices).

2.41 In the 1970s exchange rate instability, and particularly periods of weakness in the dollar, for example in 1977-78, created strong incentives for official reserve asset diversification. At first the monetary authorities of Germany, Japan and Switzerland resisted reserve roles for their currencies but the rapid growth of the Euro-markets, and also the financing needs of Germany in the late 1970s, eventually facilitated reserve diversification on a substantial scale. The share of dollars in official holdings of foreign exchange reserves declined from 78 to 68 per cent between 1973 and 1980; that of deutsche marks rose from 6 to 14 per cent, that of Japanese yen from zero to 4 per cent and that of Swiss francs from 1 to 3 per cent. The renewed strength of the dollar, however, made it again a more attractive reserve asset in the early 1980s. Reserve diversification over the period was accompanied by frequent official, as well as private, shifts into and out of reserve currencies, complicating the management of domestic monetary policies and aggravating exchange rate instability. Improved arrangements regarding official reserves and the provision of adequate international liquidity are the subject of discussion in Chapter 4.

A deteriorating environment for world trade

2.42 The GATT entered into force in 1948 as the surviving element of a still-born, much wider framework for international trade policy, embodied in the proposed International Trade Organization. Although it has made substantial progress in certain areas, there has been increasing concern with those aspects of international trade for which there was not adequate provision, for example trade in agricultural products, commodity price instability, state-trading, intra-corporate trade, restrictive business practices, trade-related investment policies and, increasingly, non-tariff measures affecting trade.

2.43 The traditional GATT insistence upon reciprocity, regardless of the relative strength of the trading partners, has been persistently challenged by the developing countries. There have also been many changes in the trading system which were not anticipated when the GATT was established and for which the limited contractual arrangements involved in the GATT had not adequately provided. Some adaptation has taken place but there is concern that the established international trading regime may be ill-suited to the resolution of the potential trade disputes of the 1980s. At the same time, the GATT's failure to respond adequately to the perceived needs and interests of developing countries encouraged the formation of another multilateral institution in the sphere of trade, the United Nations Conference on Trade and Development (UNCTAD).[1]

2.44 Among the most important unanticipated changes in the sphere of international trade has been the expansion of governmental involvement in domestic sectoral policies, which carried with it indirect implications for international exchange and bred new issues relating to 'non-tariff measures'; the growth of transnational corporate activity and the concomitant private 'management' of intra-firm trade; and the growth of preferential trading blocs. In consequence of these and other developments it has been estimated that little more than half of the value of world trade is now transacted on the basis of the unconditional mfn tariffs on which the GATT system is centred, and an even smaller proportion is at the same time transacted between independent private actors.

2.45 The most serious aspect of the decline in the proportion of trade taking place on the basis of GATT assumptions and norms has been the growing resort to non-tariff trade measures. Already used in the 1960s beyond the traditionally heavily protected agricultural and textiles sectors, these damaging forms of industrial protectionism, evading the GATT's provisions and defying its principles, were substantially extended in the 1970s and at times institutionalised. *Ad hoc,* sector-specific, discriminatory and unpredictable measures have been unilaterally or bilaterally introduced to 'order' markets, under the guise of 'voluntary export restraints', 'orderly marketing arrangements', 'industrial policies' and the like. Reduced growth and severe recession have encouraged protectionist sentiment, and there are few established rules to limit the use of the principal non-tariff instruments.

2.46 The new industrial protectionism has created major uncertainties for traders and investors while limiting the prospects for productivity

---

1. The formal purposes for which UNCTAD was set up are given in Appendix I.

growth through continuing structural change in the industrialised countries. Reduced and uncertain market access also adds to the problems developing countries face in servicing their external debt. The breakdown of 'order' in the trade regime is especially damaging to the smaller and weaker members of the international community — developing countries and the smaller industrialised ones — which are both highly trade-dependent and, because of their limited capacity to retaliate, exceptionally vulnerable. The possibilities of restoring order to a deteriorating trade scene and eventually improving the international trading regime are the subjects of attention in Chapter 7.

New issues in the energy sector

2.47 Control over raw materials, particularly oil, has always been important in the post-war international system. With the leadership of the United States (and initially also the United Kingdom), energy supplies were reasonably assured to all in the post-war years. The availability of low priced and apparently secure supplies of oil in the 1950s and 1960s facilitated rapid economic development both in the industrialised countries and in many developing countries. This development, however, involved a rapidly growing dependence of industrialised and industrialising countries on the international oil market.

2.48 With the changes in control over natural resources in the late 1960s and, especially, the early 1970s, not only did oil cease to be so low in price but confidence in the ability of the international market to offer security of supply also faded. Many oil-importers felt, in consequence, the need to ensure supply security in other ways, including the creation or strengthening of bilateral deals involving counter-trade or other arrangements with energy supply sources. Such arrangements contributed to the increased worldwide reversion to trade bilateralism. Macro-economic policies were also influenced, since for those countries, such as Japan and Korea, heavily dependent on energy imports, the need to be able to cope with substantial price increases saw balance-of-payments and exchange rate policies geared to concerns for energy supply security; such concerns also heightened sensitivity to external barriers to their manufactured exports, since these provide the foreign exchange with which to purchase oil and other essential raw material imports.

2.49 The International Energy Agency has developed an emergency oil-sharing scheme but apart from doubts as to how effective it would be in a future crisis situation, it provides only for the industrialised countries. The extension of development lending by the World Bank (and some regional banks) to energy projects contributes to the diversity of supply sources.

2.50 This Report does not address the full range of energy issues but those relating to pricing and security of supplies are discussed in Chapter 3.

Declining support for internationalism and multilateralism

2.51 Despite the widespread recognition of the growing interdependence of the world economy, recent economic troubles have inevitably weakened in some places the support for internationalism and multilateralism which underlay the Bretton Woods system. The collapse of the par-value system in 1973 was a signal of the intensifying pressures. Since then countries have been preoccupied with their own problems of recession and inflation, and the policies adopted for dealing with these problems, particularly by the United States and other major industrialised countries, have had unplanned and severe effects on other countries and on the world economy. In addition, the effects of the recession have been to increase resort to nationalistic and defensive trade policies, although the formal consensus has continued to oppose protectionism. At the theoretical level, also, there has been a natural tendency to look back over the whole post-war period and to question the basis of the Bretton Woods system in the light of subsequent developments, particularly the inflation of the last fifteen years.

2.52 The combination of defensive national policies with these ideological trends has led to some retrogression in what was by no means a fully developed state of international co-operation. Internationalism has been set back not only because of the strong domestic orientation generally given to countries' policies, but also because some urgent needs of the world economy have been neglected while countries struggled with their own problems. The most obvious of such needs have been that for the management of international liquidity, which is addressed in Chapter 4, and the need for continued international economic co-operation in assisting economic development. Little progress toward the achievement of internationally agreed aid targets is being registered. The official development assistance policies of major industrialised countries have increasingly been redirected towards their national economic and security interests, and international objectives are increasingly pursued bilaterally or with a limited number of allied countries. The share of multilateral development agencies in total ODA budgets has also been falling. One of the serious consequences of these developments is the limited international response to the desperate situation facing the low-income countries at the present time.

2.53 Reduced support for international and multilateral policies and arrangements is a problem that underlies all the discussion to follow. The specific problems of official development assistance and the multilateral agencies are discussed in Chapter 6.

Chapter 3

Recovery and Improved Stabilisation Policies for the Future

Recovery

3.1 The recession has caused massive unemployment in the industrialised countries, slow growth in the world as a whole, trading and payments problems for most primary product exporting and low-income countries, disaster for many of the poorest countries, and in 1982 a debt crisis in the international financial system. Whatever might have been the ideal international response to the second oil price rise, from which the recession may be said to date, there would inevitably have been a difficult and painful process of economic and financial adjustment. However, the recession was undoubtedly deepened by the adoption of deflationary monetary and fiscal policies by most of the major industrialised countries, as well as many others, in an attempt to absorb the income-reducing effects of the oil price rise and at the same time to reduce actual and expected inflation rates. The impact of these deflationary policies on real incomes, output and employment is evident. Commodity prices fell to very low real levels. World trade suffered a major setback. Inflation rates, and presumably expectations, in the industrialised countries proved to be more difficult to alter, and only recently has there been evidence that the actual rates are declining, although the evidence about expectations is mixed. The stubborn resistance of inflation to deflationary policies, coupled with the widespread opinion that no other available policy was effective, largely explains the persistence of governments in adhering to their policies. The main alternative policy, that of stabilising money incomes by either legal controls or less formal consensual agreement, was widely held to have been tried in the past without much success.

3.2   Recovery is a vital step towards removing the threat of a major international financial crisis with its certain promise of economic chaos, and restoring confidence in the international economic system. However, sustainable non-inflationary recovery will be difficult to achieve, and may require immediate improvements in the international financial and trading system.

3.3   Even if such a recovery were soon achieved, many of the problems of the global economy would remain. Employment is not expected to rebound with the same vigour as output, so that protectionist pressures are likely to continue. The debt-servicing obligations of the developing countries will continue to require severe domestic retrenchment, with accompanying depressing effects upon demand for others' exports. In many cases, it will be several years before the damage done to domestic living standards by current cutbacks on repair and maintenance and by the rundown of capital facilities can be made up, or enough foreign exchange freed from debt-service obligations to permit expenditure on imports required for resumed growth. Resumed global growth will also stimulate commodity price increases and the possibility of higher rates of inflation, which may generate official deflationary monetary and fiscal policies again, aborting recovery. Dissatisfaction with existing mechanisms for international economic co-operation will remain widespread.

3.4   It would be pointless to pretend there are any easy routes to recovery. In the major industrialised countries the recovery at present envisaged by agencies like the OECD and the IMF is modest. It may be just strong enough to give some relief to the rest of the world and reduce the threat of further debt crises. But it is unbalanced among major countries and its potential fragility is emphasised in all forecasts. To sustain and enhance the recovery will require effective and co-ordinated international action. In this respect it is to be hoped that the 1983 Williamsburg Declaration on Economic Recovery can be effectively translated into policy.

3.5   Macro-economic policies in the major industrialised countries should be mutually consistent in their pursuit of the accepted objectives of non-inflationary recovery. Consultations to this end should continue to ensure that the wider international effects of domestic policies are adequately taken into account in advance. Sustained recovery seems unlikely if real rates of interest remain at their current levels or rise still further. To maintain non-inflationary growth, once adequately started, it will be necessary to put a lid on anticipated sources of inflationary pressure, prevent accidental shocks and ensure continuing growth in productivity.

3.6 It is not for this Report to prescribe individual national policies relating to recovery or the maintenance of sustained non-inflationary growth. Its mandate relates purely to the international aspects of these objectives. Even these aspects of economic problems can only be properly addressed when national governments are willing to do so. International rules and institutions can ultimately function only if governments allow them to.

3.7 Co-ordinated international action must be addressed to achieve several vital preconditions for sustained and enhanced recovery. These are, above all: avoidance of an acceleration of inflation arising from international influences; avoidance of crises of international debt and liquidity; and avoidance of further moves to protectionism and competitive devaluation.

3.8 Until inflation rates have been reduced to low levels for a lengthy period it would be dangerous to assume that inflationary expectations have been substantially reduced. Furthermore, the likelihood remains that inflation would accelerate if output grew too quickly over a short period of time, hitting bottlenecks and rekindling inflationary expectations. A sharp burst of growth could accelerate increases in commodity prices with twin effects. First, the increases would improve the terms of trade of primary producing countries and provide a desirable, indeed necessary, transfer of purchasing power to them. Secondly, however, the rises could spark off further inflationary effects in the industrialised countries. It is an essential precondition for sustained, non-inflationary recovery that rises in commodity prices be absorbed in non-inflationary ways in the major industrialised countries, i.e. by offsets to 'normal' increases in real incomes.

3.9 All countries have an interest in controlling inflation and therefore in the threat of its acceleration in one another's economies. Countries with political and social structures conducive to consensual incomes policies will no doubt continue to pursue them to the envy of their neighbours. Others must continue to rely on more traditional indirect macro-economic constraining policies.

3.10 Recovery should remove some of the present impulses to intensified protectionism. However, it will affect countries' external accounts in different ways because of changes in comparative advantage and differences in inflation rates and interest rates. It is essential that recovery should not be limited or aborted by the resumption of autarkic measures or competitive devaluations. Changes in external accounts must allow for appropriate exchange rate adjustments within a co-ordinated international framework.

3.11 Crises of debt and liquidity during the recession have originated mainly in middle-income developing countries, but the threat of consequential banking failures has of course affected the major industrialised countries and through them the entire world. For some time to come, the large burden of short-term debt accumulated by many countries will be a constraint on growth, but more particularly a potential source of crisis. This is especially relevant in the immediate future, when recovery will not yet have made much impact upon many developing countries still struggling with their present foreign exchange shortages. Immediate international action will be required to deal at source with any crises as they emerge, and before the financial effects spread elsewhere (see Chapter 8).

Long-term Improvement in International Macro-economic Stabilisation

3.12 The achievement of sustained non-inflationary recovery will ease many of the pressures on the existing international financial and trading system. It may also, particularly if it results from, or is assisted by, internationally co-ordinated measures, encourage desirable permanent changes in the functioning of the system. It will not, however, of itself do away with the problems which created the crisis in the first place or overcome the longer-term need for systemic adaptation to the major changes in the international economy which were detailed in Chapter 2.

3.13 Coming after two relatively tranquil decades, the shocks and instabilities in the international economy over the past decade were largely unforeseen and were more severe than any that the basic framework of international economic institutions had previously been required to handle. A sound longer-run international economic system would not normally encounter problems as severe as those which have characterised the past few years; on the infrequent occasions when it nevertheless did, it would not impose such heavy costs upon those nations and people least able to protect themselves against externally created shocks. Prime objectives within a reformed international system must be improved stabilisation mechanisms and contra-cyclical policies, together with improved protection for those most affected when instabilities and shocks nevertheless persist. These objectives are fundamental and ongoing. Their effective attainment over the longer-run is unlikely to be purely the product of constant short-term patching and filling in response to changing events, as to some degree the engineering of a global recovery and indeed much subsequent macro-economic policy formation must be. Rather, what is required is a more deliberate construction of the elements of a more stable and equitable global economy. Reducing uncertainty and the risk of unforeseen disturbances strengthens the market system by permitting its signals to work more effectively; the resulting lengthening of planning horizons encourages orderly change and more rapid growth and development.

3.14 Stabilisation and contra-cyclical effects may be promoted both by automatic stabilising elements in national and international systems and by active discretionary policies pursued by governments and multilateral institutions. Automatic stabilising elements in the global economy may include general rules and codes of conduct for official institutions as well as the more narrowly conceived contra-cyclical mechanisms. There has been generally increased recognition of the role of automatic stabilisation devices within national economies over the past several decades. There has been little parallel growth in automatic stabilising mechanisms at the international level. One obvious area for reform is therefore to create or bolster automatic international stabilisation.

3.15 The most important elements in automatic or quasi-automatic stabilisation at the international level are those relating to the provision of stable and adequate international liquidity, and the maintenance of stable and predictable regimes for the international flow of capital, goods and services. These issues are addressed in Chapters 4 to 7. In the remainder of this section the primary concern is with other measures to stabilise the international economy, including more effective co-operation in national stabilisation policies.

3.16 Discretionary contra-cyclical policies are inherently more controversial and difficult to agree upon, not only internationally but even within nations. In part this is because of the difficulty of differentiating between cycles and trends. Disagreements also stem from different weights assigned to the costs of unemployment and inflation, or to ideological, doctrinal or judgemental differences as to the efficacy of particular policy instruments. There is certainly less confidence today than there was in the 1950s in the capacity of macro-economic policy-makers to 'fine tune' their policy decisions effectively to mitigate the cycle. That governments should seek to exert a stabilising influence upon market-based economies is nevertheless generally agreed.

3.17 The starting point for any planning for improved consultation and/or co-ordination of discretionary national contra-cyclical policies must be recognition of the twin facts of significant international interdependence and almost total national independence in policy-making. While efforts to strengthen or establish global-level multilateral institutions continue, realism requires that for the foreseeable future primary emphasis be placed upon national-level economic policy decisions. It may never be possible to achieve total agreement among governments of varying power, political persuasion and economic interest as to what economic policies are best pursued either within nations or at the international level at any particular time. But it should be possible to reduce the costs to third parties as well as to those directly involved in international disagreements; to increase the mutual consistency of national economic policies; to reduce the degree of arbitrariness and unilateralism in international economic decision-making; and to develop arrangements in which the international implications of domestic policies are more explicitly and systematically taken into account at the national level.

3.18 Even when the national policy-makers are all in basic agreement as to the overall direction of desirable global macro-economic policy — whether expansionary or deflationary — they may get the aggregate effects wrong if they each proceed individually. Whilst each national economy is an 'open' one in which there are 'leakages' in planned demand or monetary change, so reducing the size of the relevant 'multipliers', there are no such leakages from the global economy. Multipliers in the 'closed' global economy are consequently larger than in 'open' national ones. Independently formulated national deflationary or expansionary policies, when aggregated, are therefore likely to 'overshoot' agreed objectives. The urging of generalised restraint or expansion by the major powers or international bodies like the IMF may evoke policy responses which consistently miss their targets. Nor will general awareness of this problem make collectively appropriate policy formation any easier. In the absence of a global macro-economic decision-maker, consultation and co-ordination of policies at least among the major economies will be necessary if the desired objectives are to have a good chance of being attained.

3.19 When national policy-makers in major economies disagree as to the desirable direction of overall macro-economic policy change, ways must be found to permit each economy, as far as possible, to go its separate way in an ordered fashion, with a minimum degree of damage to one another or to third parties. Consultations in such cases may achieve some narrowing of differences in policy positions. In some circumstances they may make it marginally easier for individual countries to take difficult policy decisions. There is obviously no way to overcome international differences of view as to what other countries should be doing in their own or the general interest. But pre-agreed procedures, if not indeed norms or rules, may ease the inevitable continuing frictions.

3.20 Macro-economic policy co-ordination may thus take the form of rules governing the use of policy instruments; or of regular consultation as to both national and international objectives and the deployment of specific policy instruments; or both.

Improved consultation and co-ordination

3.21 Improved arrangements for consultation and co-ordination of national macro-economic policies at least among the major industrialised countries are clearly highly desirable. A principal objective in international macro-economic policy consultation and co-ordination is that of promoting smooth and equitable adjustment to international payments imbalances. The exchange rate regime is fundamental to the external adjustment process, and in a 'managed float' system, mutually consistent approaches to exchange rates are sought as a major objective. In recent years, with internationally mobile capital and more economic interdependence than ever, it has become evident that exchange rate questions cannot easily be separated from monetary, fiscal or trade policy issues. All must be considered together if policies are not to continue to work at cross-purposes.

3.22 Foreign exchange rates under the pre-1971 Bretton Woods regime are generally considered to have been too inflexible. Eventual adjustment to the realities of payments imbalance was usually accompanied by speculative capital flows and 'crises'. Increased flexibility of key currency exchange rates has therefore generally been welcomed. As has been seen, however, more flexible foreign exchange rates have been highly volatile and inclined to persistent misalignment, with potentially heavy costs in terms of overall objectives of growth, stability and openness of international exchange.

3.23 Exchange rates, an important category of prices, are only one among a number of related economic variables: inflation rates, GNP growth rates, interest rates, levels of capacity utilisation, employment, trade barriers, etc. Monetary, trade and other policies may be specifically geared to exchange rate objectives, and conversely. Agreements or interventions in foreign exchange markets cannot alone hope to influence the entire range of variables which underlie them, and may therefore not be socially very productive. Mutually consistent or co-ordinated macro-economic policies will not function to their full potential effect unless the entire range of national macro-economic objectives and policy instruments for their attainment are discussed and developed at the same time and together. By doing so and by developing mutually consistent (not necessarily 'convergent') policies based upon agreed targets for such key variables as individual nations' current accounts (and implicitly appropriate dimensions and direction of capital flows), policy-makers may contribute to the creation of a more stable and predictable overall international economic environment.

3.24 Some place particular importance upon agreements in the realm of monetary policy, and these are undoubtedly of major importance. Since national governments differ in the emphasis they place upon the use of particular macro-economic policy instruments, it is best that both fiscal and monetary policies, and the national mixes thereof, be discussed together with exchange rate and balance-of-payments issues.

3.25 Undoubtedly underplayed in recent consultations among the industrialised countries over macro-economic policies is the link between trade policies and fiscal/monetary/exchange rate actions. Within national governments as between them, these inter-relationships have typically been inadequately addressed; trade policy formation is still frequently undesirably isolated from financial and exchange rate policy discussions. The May 1983 meeting of ministers of trade and of finance of countries participating in the Williamsburg Summit is a welcome precedent, upon which further such consultations, preferably of a more multilateral character, should be built.

3.26 Improved consultation or joint policy-making arrangements should exist on a permanent basis and not merely at times of crisis or to engineer co-ordinated recovery from a particularly serious recession. Whilst global stability may seem to require that the prime participants in such improved macro-economic management arrangements among nations be the governments of the major industrialised countries (which already participate in some efforts of this kind in the Group of Five (G5), the Bank for International Settlements (BIS), Western Economic Summits and the OECD), a wider interest demands that they be to a significant degree multilateralised.

3.27 Multilateral participation in macro-economic consultations and co-ordination efforts, even when the main issues relate to the policies of a relatively few major economies, is necessary because the effects of whatever policies are agreed have ramifications far beyond the borders of the industrialised countries. Even if feedback effects from smaller economies to the more powerful ones were small (and the combined feedback effects of all smaller economies are by no means small), the universal credibility, legitimacy and ultimately stability of the global economic order depends upon universal participation in its major decision-making forums. Such multilateralised consultations obviously do not preclude the continuing process of consultation and co-ordination in a wide variety of policy issues by narrower groups of countries.

3.28 The most obvious existing multilateral forum for macro-economic consultation is the IMF. Elsewhere we argue that the World Bank is no less involved in macro-economic policy issues than the IMF, and that the trade issues now principally discussed within the GATT and UNCTAD are frequently considered in too narrow a context and underplayed in ongoing international economic policy consultations. A forum which is jointly served by the IMF, the World Bank, the GATT and the UNCTAD therefore seems most appropriate.

3.29 The 1982 Versailles Summit made a beginning in increased IMF involvement with major industrialised countries' policy formation in the pledge to strengthen their co-operation with the IMF in its surveillance work 'and to develop this on a multilateral basis taking into account particularly the currencies constituting the SDR'. Since then, the Managing Director of the Fund has participated in G5 discussions of the possibilities of better co-ordination of their macro-economic policies. At the Williamsburg Summit the intention of 'reinforcing ... multilateral co-operation with the International Monetary Fund in its surveillance activities' was accepted. IMF involvement in G5 consultations should help to focus attention on the need for consistency of policies; it could also bring a global dimension, which may be missing from limited group discussions, to bear on these consultations. This process needs to be carried much further, particularly with regard to assessing the total supply of the five major reserve currencies in relation to the world demand for them. While the IMF has separate consultations with each of these countries and it now meets with them in G5 and other discussions, truly 'multilateral consultations' do not take place as yet.

3.30 The permanent and representative Council recommended by the IMF Committee of Twenty was to 'meet regularly, three or four times a year as required and . . . have the necessary decision-making powers to supervise the management and adaptation of the monetary system, to oversee the continuing operation of the adjustment process, and to deal with sudden disturbances which might threaten the system.' By adding trade to its supervisory mandate, and authorising participation of the staff of the World Bank, UNCTAD and GATT, as well as the IMF, such a Council could serve as a permanent forum for discussion and decision-making on international trade and monetary issues. Relatively modest amendments in the operating procedures of the present advisory Interim Committee of the IMF — expanding its participation and its agenda, and increasing the frequency of its meetings — might permit an immediate start. The material prepared for the IMF's annual *World Economic Outlook,* the World Bank's annual *World Development Report,* the GATT's annual report on *International Trade* and the UNCTAD's *Trade and Development Report* could be jointly reviewed on a regular basis in such an expanded representative forum without major changes in existing staffing or support systems. Increasing its decision-making authority might take a little longer, and would have to be part of a more comprehensive rethinking of overall institutional arrangements. It may be expedient for an expanded Interim Commitee or an eventual Council to create its own committees for particular purposes such as, for instance, the surveillance of exchange rates. The sensitivities of the other international economic institutions must be considered in working out joint arrangements. What is put together to meet a specific systemic need should be seen as neither an extension of the jurisdiction of the IMF nor a reduction in the responsibilities and powers of other institutions.

Exchange rate regime

3.31 Exchange rates demand and have recently been receiving special attention. The increased mobility of private international capital and floating exchange rates, neither of which was envisaged in the original Bretton Woods conception of the international monetary system, have created problems which must be addressed whether or not macro-economic consultation or co-ordination is improved. Exchange rates do not merely reflect differential competitiveness: they have been changing substantially in recent years in response to large international differentials in rates of inflation, or differences in real national rates of interest. In a world of uncertainty, they also are the product of private expectations of future inflation rates, interest rates, and political events. The short-term volatility of exchange rates is, above all, the product of changing expectations, sometimes subject to 'bandwagon effects', which generate altered preferences for the currency composition of private assets and liabilities. A world of unstable and unpredictable national political and economic policies is bound to be a world of unstable exchange rates.

3.32 Short-term volatility of exchange rates is particularly costly to smaller firms and countries which have more difficulty and/or pay higher prices in protecting themselves from its effects. Further efforts should be made to develop forward cover or other arrangements to protect the weakest from short-term exchange risk. It does not appear to involve significant overall costs to the trade and investment activities of larger economic actors.

3.33 Despite the fact that its overall costs may not be great, there is nevertheless general agreement that pointless short-term volatility should be reduced and 'disorderly conditions' in foreign exchange markets avoided, where possible. This typically involves monetary authorities in 'leaning against the wind' in these markets. When the monetary authorities of the major industrialised countries co-operate with one another in the maintenance of orderly markets the task of each is made easier. Reciprocal credit arrangements (swaps) should be expanded as required to reduce the prospect of controls over capital movements which, necessary though they occasionally may be, are inherently undesirable, productive of further market uncertainty and, in any case, only partially effective.

3.34 The smoothing of short-term and temporary fluctuations in foreign exchange markets is quite a different issue from the more difficult objective of seeking 'appropriate' foreign exchange rates over the medium-term. Exchange rates can be said to be appropriately aligned when they generate internationally acceptable current account positions over the medium-term, say over the conventional economic cycle, without resort to unusual restraints upon trade and payments.

3.35 In making such assessments the effects of relative rates of inflation must be considered together with changes in nominal rates of exchange. Permanent reduction of global inflation would reduce the need to consider real — i.e., inflation-adjusted — rather than nominal exchange rates and might eventually even permit a return to a par value system; for the foreseeable future, however, differential rates of national inflation are likely to remain too great for this to be achieved. The best guide to appropriateness in this sense, or what some call 'fundamental economic factors', is probably the real effective exchange rate, a trade-weighted and inflation-adjusted index of changes in the relevant currency's bilateral exchange rates with other currencies. If international consultations as to macro-economic objectives include medium-term current account 'targets', they are likely to imply general ranges of desirable real effective exchange rates.

3.36 Uncertainties, imprecisions, other short-term influences and changing real influences on competitiveness (such as productivity) require that policy-makers work in terms of real effective exchange rate 'target zones', or guidelines, rather than more precise exchange rate targets. There is a clear role for the IMF in assessing and advocating specific guidelines or target zones for its major members, and keeping them under constant review, in particular those of the five members whose currencies are contained in the SDR 'basket'. By undertaking these tasks, the IMF would be exercising its mandate to undertake 'firm surveillance' over exchange rates in a much more symmetrical fashion than it has so far done. Implicitly, it would be exercising increased influence over the whole array of these countries' macro-economic policies. The IMF's recommended target zones might have to be revised in consultation bilaterally with particular countries or multilaterally, just as its positions on its borrowing countries' targets are subject to revision today.

3.37 In some instances, regional exchange rate and monetary agreements are in place which complement the wider multilateral system and do not stand in the way of its improvement. There is no reason why they should not be maintained. A partial attempt at promoting greater exchange rate stability has been made through the establishment of the European Monetary System (EMS) in 1979. It involves fixed but adjustable parities amongst the participating countries and a European Currency Unit as a common instrument for their efforts to reduce and eventually eliminate intra-European exchange rate fluctuations. The prospects of regional arrangements along the lines of the EMS in other developed areas of the world would seem to be minimal because of the overwhelming importance of the United States and Japan. However, in some parts of the developing world, regional clearing and payments arrangements offer a prospect for greater economy in reserve use and eventually closer monetary integration.

3.38 The Second Amendment of the Fund's Articles provided for a number of 'general obligations', including an undertaking by members to 'seek to promote stability by fostering orderly underlying economic and financial conditions and a monetary system that does not tend to produce erratic disruptions'. It also called for 'firm surveillance' by the Fund, to be exercised through consultation with members. Neither the members nor the Fund have been successful in fulfilling their undertakings.

3.39 Lacking the authority of a global central bank, much less that of a world government, the Fund cannot promote 'orderly underlying economic and financial conditions' unless it is armed with clear norms or rules to ensure that effective intervention does take place when disorderly market conditions develop. At present such surveillance/consultations procedures as the Fund has managed to develop are limited in their influence. Consultations between the members and the Fund take place bilaterally as well as multilaterally in the Executive Board meetings, in the Interim Committee and at the Annual Meeting. But these consultations are far too unco-ordinated and general in character to promote effective and integrated consideration of macro-economic policies on foreign exchange markets. Sensitive aspects of exchange rate and other policies, particularly those of the reserve currency countries, are discussed confidentially and usually only among the countries concerned or bilaterally with the IMF. As the Fund has to depend on the continuing willingness of these members to co-operate, and as they generally do not require its credit, its own role in developing consistent and appropriate policies tends to be limited.

3.40 A more active IMF role in exchange rate surveillance in the major industrialised countries, together with closer collaboration with other bodies in support of better multilateral macro-economic policy consultation and co-ordination (as suggested above) could be expected to promote the long-standing international objective of increased symmetry in the balance-of-payments adjustment process as between deficit countries on the one hand and surplus and reserve currency countries on the other. IMF studies and advice, buttressed by public reports if necessary and appropriate, could put more pressure than previously upon surplus and reserve currency countries to alter their policies as international adjustment requires, thereby easing the adjustment burden now borne disproportionately by deficit countries. The Committee of Twenty considered other possible means of inducing the surplus countries to share appropriately in adjustment, and an expanded IMF role as suggested here could be expected to generate further discussion and experimentation in this regard.

3.41 In the light of experience with such co-ordinated management, it might eventually be possible to bolster the exchange rate arrangements with guidelines or rules governing official interventions in support of multilaterally agreed target zones. Just as under the original Bretton Woods exchange rate regime governments undertook to maintain the values of their currencies within an agreed band about their declared parities, under a target zone system they could commit themselves to intervention to the degree or at least in the direction required to maintain real effective rates broadly within the agreed zones. Flexibility could be retained via a continuing process of review of the appropriateness of the levels and width of the agreed target zones.

3.42 An exchange rate regime highlighting guidelines or target zones for real effective exchange rates of the major currencies, as part of an improved overall system of macro-economic policy co-ordination and consultation, would constitute a significant improvement over the present disordered and anchorless exchange rate system. It cannot be emphasised too strongly however that it is probably futile to seek to develop an exchange rate regime characterised by less volatility and fewer misalignments of key currencies in the absence of improved macro-economic policy co-ordination among the major countries. In particular, joint monetary policies must be a pre-condition for a satisfactory exchange rate regime.

International price stabilisation

(i)   *Commodities*

3.43 Renewed efforts to stabilise commodity prices should be an important element in the attempt to develop more effective and more comprehensive contra-cyclical policies at the international level.

3.44 The length and depth of the recession have had a particularly destabilising effect on primary product producers. It has led to price falls of almost unprecedented severity and, with the sustained decline in economic activity, these have been highly synchronised so that there has been little possibility of offsets between commodities. According to the IMF, the average price of non-oil commodities in 1982 was 12 per cent below that of 1981 which was, in turn, 15 per cent lower than that of 1980. These falls contributed greatly to the deterioration in the terms of trade of non-oil developing countries by some 18 per cent over the last five years.

3.45 There is widespread agreement on the severely disruptive effects of undue volatility in commodity prices. These arise not just because of the influence on the domestic economies of those countries least able to deal with them, though that is important, but also because of the effects that instability has in accentuating the intensity of cycles in world economic activity.

3.46 The consequences of extreme commodity price fluctuations for debt-servicing capacity have special significance for the stability of the entire financial system upon which the industrialised as well as the developing countries depend; in the present circumstances they have contributed to the uncertainty and lack of confidence which have tended further to lower economic activity. Commodity price fluctuations are thus one means by which business cycle effects are multiplied and transmitted throughout the global economy.

3.47 A major means of achieving increased price stability for many commodities, particularly industrial raw materials, is effective macro-economic contra-cyclical policy. This would reduce the fluctuations in economic activity in the industrialised countries that give rise to the large demand shifts which are major contributors to the instability. For many commodities, domestic markets are insulated from world markets by protective barriers and any domestic instability is passed on to the international market, multiplying the initial effect. Consequently, lowered levels of protection for domestic producers and reduced government and industry interference in international commodity trade would also reduce instability.

3.48 The pursuit of non-inflationary and stable economic growth for all countries demands that the international community also pursue attempts to implement more effective mechanisms to reduce fluctuations in the prices of major products entering international trade. Such mechanisms should of course be operated in a manner consistent with allowing prices to fulfil their task of signalling the need for a reallocation of scarce resources among competing demands.

3.49 The effects of instability of commodity trade on developing country and other primary product exporters, and the need for market regulatory measures to support effective diversification measures, were fully recognised in the Havana Charter. Special provision was made by which international commodity arrangements could be negotiated to handle those problems and these were carried through into subsequent trade and other economic arrangements. The limited progress under those arrangements, the consequences of the effective exclusion of agriculture from the GATT trading rules, and the absence of measures to deal with transnational corporate and industry-based arrangements affecting commodity markets were among the important issues that led to the demand for UNCTAD. In the early 1970s UNCTAD developed a proposal for a comprehensive policy programme to deal with primary commodity trade — the Integrated Programme for Commodities (IPC) — including the establishment of a Common Fund to finance international commodity agreements (ICAs) and related arrangements for individual commodities.

3.50 At the time the UNCTAD resolution on the IPC was adopted in 1976, developing countries had considerable hopes that it would lead to constructive action; but despite agreement in 1980 to establish the Common Fund, subsequent achievements have been very limited. It has been difficult to get governments to take other than a short-term, narrowly commercial, view of ICAs or the IPC. Exporters are not particularly interested in ICAs in periods of high prices, any more than importers are in periods of low prices. Only one new ICA with price-stabilisation provisions (that for natural rubber) has been negotiated since the IPC was agreed. Moreover, the agreed size and functions of the Common Fund are much smaller than in the original conception. The negotiation of new ICAs with price-stabilisation provisions will continue therefore to be extremely difficult. Those which already exist, frequently with inadequate producer or consumer participation, have proved difficult to administer, have had insufficient finance and have been of limited effect.

3.51 The IPC has not, therefore, been effective so far in averting shocks to countries with a high dependence on commodity exports. Implementation of the Common Fund would go some way towards assisting with the financing problems and it should receive wider support than it has done so far. But, since its resources are small, it would not be adequate on its own. The search needs to be continued for new mechanisms that would be less difficult to negotiate and administer. The IMF could, for instance, consider financing nationally-held stocks in a variety of carefully defined circumstances rather than only doing so, as at present, in connection with ICAs. The aim is to find a process that has adequate safeguards for legitimate interests in the market without having to wait for the extremely slow and deliberate pace typical of the development of most ICAs. The international economic system has shown that it is sometimes able to act quickly and substantially in the financial field when necessary, but it has not yet shown equivalent capacity with respect to issues at least as serious in the commodities field.

3.52 In the longer-run, adequate financing could make an important contribution to price stabilisation efforts. Since national governments have not shown great willingness to provide finance, other methods of financing need to be explored, for example from commercial sources combined with the IMF or the multilateral development banks. Long-term contractual supply arrangements between producers and consumers are also worth pursuing though experience has emphasised the difficulties involved. Eventually, it might be possible to consider international arrangements to guarantee a minimum real price to low-income exporters of particular commodities; however, financial mechanisms to achieve the same effect, for example the import stabilisation scheme discussed below, are more likely to command support.

(ii)   *Food*

3.53 In relation to food prices, efforts to establish an International Grains Arrangement (IGA) which would provide for the use of stocks to stabilise supplies and reduce price fluctuations have similarly made little progress. These efforts need to continue, given the importance of stable grain prices. Nevertheless, international arrangements to deal with world food problems require more than an IGA. Provisions for food aid must be closely integrated with such arrangements and although to some extent they already are, under the Food Aid Convention of the International Wheat Agreement, better co-ordination is required. At present, not only do existing international arrangements not ensure increased food aid in periods of shortages and high prices for grains, but food aid tends to decline precisely during such periods of shortage. International arrangements in respect of food need to aim at co-ordinated efforts to increase food price stability, to develop welfare arrangements to provide minimum supplies of food to the malnourished and most needy groups, and to provide emergency reserves to meet disaster requirements.

(iii)   *Oil*

3.54 Petroleum remains by far the most important item in world commodity trade. The large movements in its price have created the two greatest short-term shocks to the global economy during the last ten years.

3.55 The 1973-74 oil price rise had several causes. In part a response to increasing inflation, the oil-exporters' action did have the salutary effect of reminding the oil-importing countries that they were consuming at an increasing rate a non-renewable resource whose proven reserves were being run down at a pace which many felt to be alarming. Equally important was its further stimulus to inflation, which helped lead to the recession of 1974-75. The second oil price shock of 1979-80 led not only to deep recession but also to a sharp decline in oil consumption in the industrialised countries, an expansion in non-OPEC oil production, and eventually to a fall in OPEC prices. These events caused great strains to the institutional mechanisms which had to accommodate the necessary adjustments to payments imbalances and other developments in the world financial system. Recently the direct negative macro-economic repercussions of oil price changes have been felt primarily by the oil-exporting countries, particularly Mexico, Nigeria and Venezuela. During the last ten years, therefore, both exporters and importers have suffered from the movements of oil prices and both have cause to seek a stabilising arrangement. Yet despite much discussion of the need, there is still no international arrangement between exporters and importers to help to smooth price changes and avoid the sharp and sudden movements which have characterised the oil market.

3.56 The present time has many advantages for seeking an oil price stabilisation arrangement. The prolonged recession in the oil market has reduced the gap between OPEC prices and the production costs of other sources of oil and alternative forms of energy. Because there is therefore no longer the scope for vast increase in OPEC prices, its members have an immediate interest in arrangements to achieve stability. These will be much more effective if they include importers as well as exporters. The chances of importer co-operation have improved since the major energy consuming countries, concerned now to defend the value of the huge investments they have made in the production of high cost energy and in the development of energy conservation devices, have themselves acquired a new interest in oil price stability.

3.57 It is specially important that the present oil surplus should not mislead governments into a false sense of security. Being non-renewable, the commodity is a wasting asset and serious disruptions in its supply as a result of political or military activity, not unknown in the past, cannot be ruled out in the future; moreover, in the medium-term at least, future increases in energy demand cannot be fully met without a large reliance on oil. Demand for energy by industrialised countries will almost certainly turn upwards quite significantly if there is a sustained economic recovery, particularly in heavy industry; and most developing countries are still at the stage of development when their energy consumption rises faster than their

GDP. Despite the present excess capacity in oil production, it seems likely that later in the decade fairly modest increases in energy demand may not be satisfied unless oil production rises faster than at present appears probable. In other words, because supply gaps remain a threat (and because stock managers know it and may therefore feed speculative purchases into a fairly tight market), so does the possibility of an oil price explosion. A stabilising arrangement for oil could be an important part of an international financial and trading system which is supportive of global economic stability and growth.

3.58 Massive conservation efforts and vastly increased resort to non-OPEC sources of supply by importing countries have together tended to reduce dependence on OPEC. Increased stability in OPEC-dominated oil transactions would nevertheless significantly stabilise the overall outlook for world energy supplies. Notwithstanding the many difficulties, new discussions should therefore be held between the major oil-exporting and importing countries with a view to seeking an oil price stabilisation arrangement, perhaps as part of a wider package of policies to encourage increased OPEC investments in developing countries. Failing such an arrangement, governments and the International Energy Agency will have to develop multilateral stock management and supply security arrangements of their own as best they can.

Stabilisation and support for those most affected by instability

3.59 Protection from the full effects of global economic shocks outside the control of countries is necessary for those countries which would be most affected, if they are to have an economic environment conducive to growth and development. It is particularly important for the most vulnerable countries — the poorest and those which, although possessing quite reasonable average incomes, are small, undiversified, and therefore peculiarly exposed to the vicissitudes of the world economy.

3.60 To some extent, shocks in developing countries from the instability of commodity, food and energy prices may be reduced by international commodity agreements. But not only have these proved difficult to establish and operate; they can also be of limited significance to the particular circumstances of an individual country. Export earnings from a crop can plummet as a result of harvest failure even though world market prices are stabilised through an agreement. For the exporting countries concerned, direct compensation through export earnings stabilisation arrangements may be a more effective answer.

3.61 Ideally, the most vulnerable type of country should be able to draw on a facility from which it obtains compensatory external financial resources when events beyond its control cause foreign exchange earnings to fall in real terms. The poorest countries have been the most severely buffeted by fluctuations in the terms of trade during the last ten years. They are also the countries which, because of their level of development, have the greatest difficulty in undertaking rapid reallocations and adjustments in response to external change. During the recession the severe deterioration in their terms of trade, limited adjustment capability, and inadequate access to temporary credit have meant severe cutbacks in the utilisation of their existing capacity, unnecessary depreciation in their capital stocks, and sharp reductions in income and investment, all of which even a vigorous and sustained world recovery will take some years to make up.

3.62 Particularly for the poorest countries, it would be desirable to establish a broad type of mechanism which stabilises import capacity, protecting them from fluctuations in export earnings or import prices beyond their control. For these countries, shortfalls should be made up by grants in a manner somewhat analogous to the Lome Convention's Stabex scheme for African, Caribbean and Pacific (ACP) member countries. A programme to achieve this purpose should be a matter of high international priority.

Chapter 4

International Liquidity and the IMF

Introduction

4.1   A stable, open and equitable international economic system depends upon the availability of adequate liquidity for all its member countries. Machinery for its provision is a fundamental requirement of an effectively functioning international monetary system. While adjustment is necessary in cases of fundamental disequilibrium, governments should not have to adopt deflationary macro-economic or restrictive trade policies in response to temporary balance-of-payments difficulties. The inadequacy of short-term finance can severely damage not only the countries directly experiencing balance-of-payments difficulties but also other countries with which they trade and compete for goods and capital, and thus the entire global economy. Indeed, inadequate liquidity can breed a cumulative process of competitive devaluation, protectionism and beggar-my-neighbour policies, as all struggle to restore national balance in difficult global circumstances. The experience of the 1930s demonstrated the dreadful possibilities for such downward spirals, and dramatised the need for a more rational system of global liquidity creation and management. The continuing problems of liquidity provision, associated with those of international stability discussed in the previous chapter, contribute to failures in international efficiency as well as having adverse effects on the equity of the international system.

4.2   There is no more crucial area of international monetary policy than that relating to ensuring an adequate and appropriately distributed supply of international liquidity. Too little liquidity could abort global recovery and even bring on depression; too much could reignite inflation. The discussion that follows will therefore address both the immediate policy needs and the longer-run systemic requirements for the provision of liquidity.

4.3 Countries, like companies and individuals, need a sufficient supply of liquidity if they are to conduct their affairs in an orderly way and plan for growth. Since it is not possible perfectly to synchronise international payments and receipts, countries must have access to a 'buffer stock' of internationally acceptable financial assets so as to meet obligations that may fall due before offsetting claims are met. Liquidity can be provided in a variety of ways: (i) owned-reserves, for example gold, holdings of reserve currencies (now including deutsche marks, yen, Swiss francs and other currencies as well as dollars), reserve position in the IMF; (ii) ready access to official sources of finance, such as low-conditionality IMF credit, intergovernmental swaps and credit lines, etc.; and (iii) for the commercially creditworthy, up to certain limits, credit facilities from commercial banks. Since owned-reserves are under a country's own control they provide a firmer basis for domestic policy management than do credit facilities. IMF credit offered on conditional terms, together with other conditional credits from the BIS, governments, or other sources, may be considered part of a country's overall potential liquidity; but, since it cannot be counted upon and is not as fast-disbursing, this potential credit does not provide actual liquidity in the same sense as owned-reserves or low-conditionality credit.

4.4 This chapter deals with owned-reserves and access to IMF credit (both low-conditionality and high-conditionality) and other comparable official sources of finance; the next chapter is concerned with commercial bank finance; and the following one with longer-term finance. The lines between these three categories are not completely clearcut, and we start with some general consideration of the present adequacy of liquidity.

Adequacy of Liquidity

4.5 Traditional discussions of the adequacy of liquidity have tended to focus on its role in lubricating commercial transactions. The need for liquidity arises because of seasonal variations in shipments and fluctuations in export earnings or import expenditures, which lead to mismatches between international receipts and payments. A common measure of the adequacy of a country's liquidity has been the ratio between its owned-reserves and its imports of goods and services.

4.6 However, after the first oil crisis, the commercial banks, in the absence of responsive official financing and faced with depressed domestic demand for funds, expanded into the international arena in a major way. This development rendered simple measures of the above kind less helpful in assessing the overall liquidity position of some countries.

4.7　Access to international credit through the commercial banks has until recently provided many countries with a fairly ready and substantial, albeit volatile, source of liquidity to augment owned-reserves. At the same time, however, the build-up of foreign obligations has brought with it debt-service requirements that for many countries have become large in relation to revenue from commercial transactions. The innovation of floating interest rate debt together with the volatibility of international interest rates in the last four years has increased the variability of interest payments in an unpredictable way. Furthermore, even in favourable conditions in credit markets, factors such as a bunching of maturities may make it difficult for a country promptly to refinance maturing medium- and long-term debt. Additional liquidity may be necessary in current circumstances to cover interest payments and possibly to bridge the gap between the repayment of the existing debt and the contracting of a new loan. At the same time, the last decade has seen increased instability in many countries' terms of trade, longer recessions and sharper 'shocks' to the balance-of-payments, all of which demand greater liquidity for the achievement of a given degree of stability in import volume.

4.8　These considerations point to the need for a broader measure of the adequacy of liquidity. At a minimum it should take into account all the sources of usable finance on which a country may reasonably expect to draw in cases of payments difficulties. As well as owned-reserves, unused bank credit lines and potential access to low-conditionality IMF credit, including SDRs, must be included. At the same time, such a measure must relate these not only to 'normal' payments for imports of goods and services but also to required debt-service payments; and, though more difficult, it should take account of such factors as the changing degree of instability in external receipts and payments, and the compressibility of imports.

4.9　In judging the adequacy of liquidity, it is possible to make global calculations of liquidity in relation to imports. It is important to note that gold, if valued at market prices, now amounts to about half of the world's total reserves; and that gold price increases have vastly enlarged total measured liquidity in the 1970s. But gold held as reserves is highly concentrated, with five countries accounting for two-thirds of the total, and even these countries are unlikely to use their gold to any great extent to settle international transactions. For most practical purposes, a better indication of the adequacy of global liquidity is obtained, therefore, by leaving gold out of account.

4.10 While, on average, non-gold reserves (in dollar terms) increased at a rate of 18 per cent per annum between 1971 and 1980 (compared with 10 per cent per annum during 1951-70), between 1980 and 1982 they fell by 10 per cent. For the world as a whole, they amounted to 11 weeks' worth of imports of goods at the end of 1982, compared with 15 weeks at the end of 1971. If services are included, the decline is considerably larger, particularly for developing countries; total non-gold reserves of non-oil developing countries amounted at the end of 1982 to only 7 weeks of their imports of goods and services, down from 12 weeks in 1977-78 and 8 to 9 weeks in 1974-75.

4.11 This large, sharp decline in global reserves, together with the drying up in commercial bank financing to developing countries, would suggest that it has become a matter of urgency to increase liquidity. One way to do this would be to resume allocations of SDRs (see paragraphs 4.35-4.39).

4.12 The urgency is reinforced by the maldistribution of reserves between countries, particularly the inadequacy of both owned-reserves and access to commercial bank credit by the poorer countries. The major developing country borrowers from the banks are middle-income and newly industrialising countries (such as Brazil, Argentina and South Korea) and the oil-exporters (such as Venezuela, Mexico, Nigeria and Algeria). The low-income countries are almost wholly reliant for external finance not just on official flows, but on concessional financing. As far as liquidity is concerned, they must rely on owned-reserves and IMF credit.

The Role of the IMF

4.13 Liquidity creation, its composition and distribution, though central to any international economic system, followed little logical or systematic pattern in the post-war years. The IMF has never fully controlled the supply of international liquidity. Nor is it likely to do so — as long as national currencies are employed as reserves. What is at issue is the degree of IMF influence over the supply of liquidity.

4.14 If there is to be increased stability and predictability in the provision of international liquidity, the most obvious mechanism to use is the IMF which was originally established, in large part, for that very purpose. Under the Bretton Woods exchange rate regime, liquidity was principally determined by the accidents of US balance-of-payments experience, in which other countries' policies, as well as those of the United States itself, played important roles. Commercial bank lending

47

to sovereign governments constituted the most important new source of expanded liquidity in the post-1971 period. Debt problems and cutbacks in commercial bank lending in 1982-83 have forced a reconsideration of the role the banks should and can play in the provision of future global liquidity requirements. As has been seen (paragraph 2.40), SDRs supplied only 5 per cent of total non-gold official reserves at the end of 1982. When net IMF disbursements to non-oil developing countries reached an unprecedented peak of $6.3 billion in 1982, they still provided only a small proportion of the total increase in these countries' current account deficits during 1980-82, or of the vastly reduced total commercial bank lending to them of $20 billion in 1982. (The IMF's share of financing the deficits in 1983 is, however, likely to be somewhat larger.) Not only must the longer-term decline in the relative importance of IMF-created liquidity be arrested, but conscious effort must be made to restore and consolidate the IMF in its appropriate place at the centre of the global liquidity system.

4.15 Admittedly, the IMF's real influence is not fully represented by a simple analysis of its contribution to financing requirements. Its seal of approval, implied by the granting of a standby arrangement after discussion with a country about its economic plans, is an important factor in encouraging private capital flows to the country in question. During the past year the IMF has been at the very centre of emergency packages negotiated among commercial banks, central banks, the BIS and debtor governments. It also influences sources of official development assistance, Paris Club official debt rescheduling and World Bank structural adjustment lending, each of which is considered later in this Report.

IMF Practices and Resources

4.16 The IMF, in keeping with its charter, has assisted its member states to absorb unavoidable internal and external shocks in an orderly manner, without resorting to measures unduly 'destructive of national or international prosperity'. It has also shown ingenuity in adjusting to changed circumstances without losing sight of its basic rationale. Thus, in response to the two oil crises, it developed special arrangements — the 'Oil Facility', the Extended Fund Facility, the Trust Fund, the Subsidy Account, the Supplementary Financing Facility and the enlarged access policy.[1]

4.17 Similarly, the IMF has responded promptly and constructively in recent months to the serious debt problems of major developing

---

1. The enlarged access policy, which applies to standby or extended arrangements, enables a member to draw up to 150 per cent of quota annually or 450 per cent over three years.

countries — problems which, as has been seen, were compounded by the recession and high rates of real interest. The eighth review of IMF quotas was accelerated and an agreement quickly reached to increase quotas by 47.5 per cent to SDR 90 billion. As a partial corrective to what many consider to be the rather moderate increase agreed in quotas, the General Arrangements to Borrow (GAB) have been expanded from SDR 6.4 billion to SDR 17 billion; and it has been agreed, provided that the IMF faces an 'exceptional situation in which balance-of-payments problems of members threaten the stability of the international monetary system', to make GAB resources available for use by all members of the Fund.

4.18 These are clearly desirable and creditable initiatives. It is necessary now to follow them up to make sure that their beneficial effects, particularly in boosting confidence, are quickly and fully realised. The first priority is for prompt legislative action to make the quota increase effective as early as possible and certainly not later than the end of 1983.

4.19 The conditions under which the enlarged and more widely usable GAB funds would actually be made available are not entirely clear. It is important that, like other resources borrowed by the Fund from its members, they should be available to all members on equal terms as a normal supplement to IMF resources. Otherwise, the sensible extension of the use of GAB funds to all Fund members would lose all meaning and in fact create apprehensions which could undermine confidence in the Fund's impartiality. For the same reason, while the Group of Ten may have prior consultations with the Fund before GAB funds are utilised, the initiative for their use should rest with the Fund management, and every effort should be made to ensure that the decisions to use them are made in spirit as well as in form by the Fund's Executive Board.

4.20 It would seem that the resources currently available to the Fund may not be adequate to meet foreseeable needs during the period before the activation of the new quotas. The Fund has already committed all its borrowed resources, although approximately SDR 10 billion was available from its ordinary resources at mid-1983. It is estimated that it will need to borrow an additional SDR 6 billion by the end of the year. There is also considerable doubt as to the adequacy of the Fund's resources, even after the quota increase and the expansion of the GAB, for the performance of its traditional functions in the longer-run. The Managing Director of the Fund is currently negotiating for more borrowed funds from member governments to tide it over until the new quotas are in place. For the longer-term, the Fund should be empowered to borrow from capital markets. Necessary preliminary agreements among members and provisional arrangements for such borrowing must be concluded so that private funds could be mobilised, if necessary, without delay. The framework for such borrowing, even if it is to be considered in rather exceptional circumstances, should therefore be erected now. (In an emergency the Fund might also resort to gold sales and/or further borrowing from its major members.)

4.21 Ultimately, the appropriate means of expanding IMF resources must be quota expansion, as decided by its Executive Board. The adequacy of IMF resources should not be determined in a circular fashion by tailoring calculations of requirements according to the amounts that it has been able to mobilise through quota increases at any given time. Nor should conditionality, which is discussed at greater length below, vary by chance according to the adequacy of IMF usable resources. All possibilities of borrowing by the Fund must be kept open, even though the preferred route for raising its resources continues to be through adequate quota increases.

4.22 The procedures for quota reviews themselves need serious reconsideration. Reviews every five years, together with inhibitions about raising quotas by more than 50 per cent or so at a time, have meant that Fund quotas have consistently lagged behind the growth of world trade. Other things being equal, it is reasonable to assume that the need for liquidity grows roughly in proportion to the growth in trade and payments. As it is, in a period of increasing trade instability, IMF quotas as a proportion of the value of world trade have shrunk drastically over the last two decades, falling from 12 per cent in 1960 to under 4 per cent today. Such trends might be avoided by a triennial review of quotas or by an agreement to increase them at some pre-agreed rate related to the growth of world trade and payments for up to, say, ten years at a time, with additional selective increases negotiated, say, once in five years.

4.23 In this connection, it should be noted that there is widespread dissatisfaction with the current formula which was devised at the end of the Second World War and therefore reflected the perceptions and power balances of almost forty years ago. Dissatisfaction with the size and distribution of quotas and the rationale for them lies behind the introduction of special arrangements like the Compensatory Financing Facility, and the policy of enlarged access. The future evolution of such arrangements cannot be judged in isolation from the question of the adequacy of quotas in the aggregate and the equity of their relative distribution.

4.24 For many countries the recently agreed 47.5 per cent increase in total quotas will mean in fact a much smaller rise in their own quotas.

For example, in the case of many Commonwealth developing countries it will be of the order of only 25 to 40 per cent. Such quota increases are smaller than those required merely to compensate for the erosion in their real value that has already been caused by inflation. They do not even make up for 1982's decline in reserves and access to bank credit. In order to retain confidence in the IMF's capacity to influence its members' liquidity there should be no change in the present policies regarding maximum access to quotas. Within that maximum, the Fund must naturally continue to exercise its judgement and discretion about what might be appropriate in any given case.

IMF-Created Liquidity

4.25 The terms upon which IMF credit is made available to member countries have always been debated, but have recently become matters of major controversy. Beyond the first credit tranche (beyond 50 per cent of quotas in the case of the Compensatory Financing Facility) and the utilisation of SDRs, IMF credit is dependent upon the meeting of certain pre-conditions, and often the subsequent attainment of quarterly performance targets. The need for conditions to be imposed, once borrowing extends beyond basic levels at which liquidity should be internationally provided, is not seriously questioned. Ideally, there should be an array of conditionalities, rising in their stringency as credits increase, as do IMF charges. What is at issue is: (i) how much of the IMF credit should be provided as true (low-conditionality) liquidity and how much on conditional terms; and (ii) when conditions are required, what they ought to be.

4.26 It is important, first, to underline the generalised need for expanding liquidity as the overall value of international exchange and the absolute size of prospective disruptions in the orderly flow of payments and receipts increase; and the fact that only reliable and fast-disbursing credit constitutes 'true' liquidity. Assuming that in some base period IMF quotas portrayed member countries' potential liquidity needs, the availability of low-conditionality IMF credit (including SDRs) should, at a minimum, thereafter expand at a rate roughly equivalent to that of the growth of the value of international payments. For the IMF to acquire an increasing role in the provision of international liquidity, this expansion would have to be faster.

4.27 As has been seen, IMF quotas have not kept pace with growth in the value of world trade since the prosperous early 1960s. Nor have SDR allocations made up the difference. Commercial bank credit expansion has undoubtedly made up some of the 'gap', but only for those countries with access to it; and its continued availability, even for those, has now been placed in some doubt. Many countries without access to commercial bank finance have been forced into inappropriate import cutbacks and resort to upper credit tranche borrowing from the IMF. For this set of reasons, the poorer countries require more low-conditionality IMF credit than they have been getting.

Reform of the Compensatory Financing Facility

4.28 In order to provide more liquidity for the poorest countries, the IMF's Compensatory Financing Facility (CFF) seems the most obvious existing mechanism upon which to build. The CFF compensates to some degree for the failure to stabilise commodity prices or to protect the import capacity of the most vulnerable countries against shock. It does this principally by helping to offset the consequences of temporary fluctuations in export earnings caused by external events. Because it is formula-based, its low-conditionality provisions do not create any accompanying problems of moral hazard. It has not in recent years provided nearly sufficient funds. In 1982, net drawings from the CFF amounted only to about one-tenth of the collective shortfall of the capital-importing developing countries, estimated on the basis of the current IMF procedures, and a much smaller proportion of those of some of the poorest countries. It could, however, make a more appropriate contribution with only modest amendments.

4.29 CFF drawings were always limited to specific quota-related maxima, rather than being related to the size of externally created balance-of-payments shocks. As IMF quota expansion lagged further behind the growth in the value of international trade and as the impact of external fluctuations increased, this fundamental limitation became ever more important. Also limiting was the IMF's failure to allow, in the calculation of shortfalls eligible for CFF credit, for import price changes (except since 1981 for temporary excesses in cereal import prices). Repayment obligations have also been more rigid in their scheduling than a facility of this purpose would seem to require, involving payments in recent years which have frequently coincided with periods of severe balance-of-payments stress. There have been no adjustments either in the application of the formula for calculating shortfalls or in terms of repayment in response to the unusual length of the recession. At the same time, CFF credit has in recent years become more closely associated with IMF conditionality, not only because of the inadequacy of quota expansion but also because of the increasing practice of linking CFF drawings with the acceptance of upper credit tranche IMF credit.

4.30 The increase in quotas proposed under the Eighth General Review will, when implemented, certainly help to expand CFF resources, but by itself it is insufficient. There will still be an urgent requirement to raise very substantially the limit of drawings, if limit there must be, as a proportion of the newly enlarged quotas. Preferable would be new rules by which CFF drawings are related to calculated shortfalls rather than to quotas. For the poorest and most vulnerable developing countries, if a mechanism such as that suggested in paragraph 3.62 is not introduced, the CFF could provide credit to the full amount of the calculated shortfall; since the overall needs of these countries are small in absolute terms, such a reform would not require large extra funding.

4.31 Secondly, the terms on which assistance is given should be made more appropriate to fulfilling the prescribed task. In so far as the CFF is designed solely to compensate for temporary shortfalls in export earnings, conditionality has no relevance; CFF credit should be offered on a virtually automatic basis. Similarly, there should be greater flexibility in the repayment period. To take account of the possibility of longer cycles this should be lengthened from the present three to five years to, say, four to ten years. Repayment obligations should also be symmetrically phased, where appropriate, in response to the changing external fortunes of the borrowing country — which are no more the responsibility of the borrower than was the external shock which motivated resort to the CFF in the first place. For the poorer developing countries, again if the mechanism proposed in paragraph 3.62 fails to materialise, a degree of concessionality by means of subsidised interest payments should also be introduced.

4.32 Thirdly, the formula for calculating export-earnings shortfalls should be revised to take greater account of changes in import prices; as a start, import prices of fuels might be added to those of cereals in such determinations. There is ultimately no reason why an overall index of import prices could not be devised for use in every developing country, no matter how weak its present domestic statistical system. Longer cycles would also call for a revised means of calculating shortfalls; greater flexibility in the application of the current five-year moving average formula would reduce the risk that calculated shortfalls decline in long recessions. A more ambitious reform would involve calculating shortfalls against agreed projections of export earnings.

4.33 These modifications would certainly make the CFF more expensive to operate than at present, but they are needed if any serious attempt is to be made to provide adequate liquidity for those that need it most and, more generally, to assist developing countries to stabilise their imports. The limited nature of the reforms suggested implies that finance should not prove an insuperable problem even in the short-term. Since the conditions of recession, when the largest aggregate shortfalls in export earnings are likely to take place, are those in which increased liquidity creation is least likely to be inflationary, SDR allocations seem an obvious contra-cyclical and non-inflationary means of financing expanded CFF activities. Eventually, an IMF with appropriately revised quotas and/or the capacity to furnish SDRs as required would be able to meet the needs of countries now dependent upon an expanded CFF.

4.34 As a logical extension of the argument for an improved CFF, the IMF should similarly provide countries confronted with a non-reversible adverse external shock, particularly those without access to other sources of credit, with the right to low-conditionality finance to assist them to adjust to it. A definite period of time within which to adjust could be specified and their governments subjected to implicit pressure to do so. Such an arrangement might offer finance which is made available to a country on a *tapering basis* over, say, a four-year period. The country would be allowed automatic borrowing rights equivalent to 100 per cent of the estimated current account effect of the non-reversible adverse shock in the first year, with progressively smaller credit allocations in succeeding years. Failure to take advantage of the financing opportunity so provided to design and implement an adjustment programme would force the country into recourse to the IMF's high-conditionality facilities. Procedures for the handling of such structural adjustments are considered at greater length below (paragraphs 4.49-4.57).

The Role of SDRs

4.35 In addition to the regular consideration of the adequacy of IMF quotas and the reconsideration of the basis for their inter-country distribution, both recommended above (paragraphs 4.22-4.24), it is important that annual allocations of SDRs on the basis of (eventually revised) quotas resume forthwith. These allocations should be on an unconditional basis and are needed as a supplement to the present level of liquidity, to improve the composition of reserves and as a step towards a more orderly and predictable liquidity creation system. If from time to time there were an excess of liquidity, SDR allocations can continue via the establishment of a Substitution Account.

4.36 At present there is insignificant prospect of further SDR allocations creating a danger of accelerating world inflation. For example, an allocation of SDR 10 billion could add no more than 1/100 of one per cent to global aggregate demand, an amount also most unlikely, even if it were substantially larger, to stimulate inflationary expectations significantly. For SDR allocations to play their full role in the IMF's effort to influence international liquidity, there should be appropriate variations from year to year and more streamlined decision-making procedures.

4.37 The objective of a single-currency reserve system based on the SDR remains a desirable one for the longer term. Despite the apparent reversion at present to a multi-currency system, with all its attendant dangers and inequities, it is important not to lose sight of that aspiration in the formation of current international monetary policies. Some measures have been taken and still others are possible in its furtherance.

4.38 The SDR is increasingly being used outside the Fund as a unit of account. Fourteen international and regional organisations and various international conventions now use it to express monetary magnitudes. So far there has been only very limited use of SDRs (or other 'baskets') for invoicing internationally traded goods. This reflects partly the lack of familiarity with the SDR and its potential advantages but, probably more importantly, the limited facilities available for making direct payments in SDRs. Whenever SDRs are used they must be converted into a 'vehicle' currency first. Authorisation for private holding of SDRs, the creation of SDR clearing arrangements and the fostering of an inter-bank market in SDRs would make their use more attractive. Greater use of the SDR as a unit of account would itself increase the demand for direct settlement arrangements and hence the incentive for such a development. Co-operation involving central banks and the IMF could, as suggested earlier (paragraph 3.36), help to reduce exchange rate fluctuations between the five currencies constituting the SDR; this would also help materially in increasing its use in private transactions.

4.39 Ultimately more important to an IMF-based liquidity system than any of these extensions in SDR usage would be the merger of the IMF's General Account, which relates to normal drawings, with its Special Drawing Rights Account. Such a consolidation of IMF credit provision would greatly simplify IMF lending, avoid the need for national currencies in IMF operations, and open the way to its playing a role more like that of a global central bank, with the capacity to create liquidity as required.

IMF Conditional Credit

4.40 Controversy arises over the nature of the conditions attached to IMF loans; wrongly handled, conditionality can actually diminish discipline and delay necessary adjustments by encouraging countries to postpone going to the IMF until they are in severe trouble. More irksome adjustment is then required — and hence more irksome conditionality, further complicating the already complex relationship between the borrower and the conditional lender. There is also the possibility that inappropriate conditions may create unnecessary deflation and import cutbacks. To encourage early recourse to the IMF, it should offer its financial support on a suitable basis for the adjustment period in prospect, on the basis of relevant conditionality, as agreed at UNCTAD VI.

4.41 The detailed nature of conditionality, when it is applied, varies considerably from case-to-case. The IMF's guidelines on conditionality are sufficiently general to leave room for substantial discretion in individual lending circumstances.

4.42 A study by the Fund of upper credit tranche arrangements between 1971 and 1980 concluded that significant improvements in the balance-of-payments were generally achieved, rates of inflation were less than the average for non-oil developing countries and, although declines in the deficit reflected increased domestic savings, real rates of consumption did not fall by much. More recent evidence suggests that Fund programmes often have limited effectiveness. Particularly is this the case in the low-income countries. Although the programmes frequently tend to move the various statistical indicators in the desired direction, they generally have only a short-term impact; IMF programme targets are often missed, and programmes are subject to fairly frequent breakdowns. The construction of effective adjustment policies is a matter of difficult judgement as to both political and economic questions. There are rarely unambiguous answers to the problems of countries experiencing balance-of-payments difficulties, and it is usually fruitless and unproductive to hold that there are. It should not therefore be surprising that there have been so many instances of acrimonious dispute between the IMF and the governments of borrowing countries. IMF programmes are most likely to be effective when they are genuinely adopted as 'their own' by borrowing governments.

4.43 It cannot be said too often that the conditions and timing of successful balance-of-payments adjustment programmes vary from country to country, as between different time periods, and according to the causes of the original payments imbalances.

4.44 The specifics of conditionality — and this applies to the World Bank as well as to the IMF — should be made more appropriate to the borrower's own situation. They must recognise that when several objectives have to be met in a changing environment, the same policy mix will not be appropriate in every case. The emphasis on demand or supply-side management should aim at minimising the costs imposed on the country concerned. Productive investment must escape as far as possible the brunt of the cuts, and it may sometimes be necessary to go slow in achieving ultimately desirable objectives, such as a reduction in subsidies. The performance targets (which are so often missed) could be specified with agreed margins of deviation; they might even be replaced by broader assessments of economic policy and performance. Inadequate performance, however defined, would trigger a review mission whose brief would be to form an overall view of progress and would not necessarily lead to curtailment of lending.

4.45 Although weighted voting may be relevant when it comes to basic policy (size of quotas, SDR allocations, etc.), it has little relevance when deciding what are the appropriate policies for a country to follow in a particular situation. A self-denying ordinance simply to debate, discuss and advocate when conditionality in adjustment programmes is under consideration would do much to reduce political heat and bring the whole conditionality question back on to a mutually more responsive and constructive track.

4.46 Where conditions and performance targets are agreed or imposed, future dispute would be minimised by the use of targets which not only are sensitive to these issues but also relate primarily and directly to the capacity of the borrowers to repay. This implies primary reliance on balance-of-payments targets rather than monetary ones, and the minimisation of external prescriptions as to the precise character of domestic credit and fiscal management. It would also be sensible and conducive to improved relations between the IMF and its borrowers if performance targets, particularly in multi-year programmes where projections must be more doubtful, were themselves linked in a pre-agreed fashion to key exogenous determinants of performance such as the real prices of the principal exports or the overall terms of trade.

4.47 There is a case for altering the stringency of conditionality of IMF lending in accordance with the global economy's requirements. Some contra-cyclical IMF activity is already implicit in the above recommendations for stabilising the provision of liquidity and reforming the Compensatory Financing Facility. It may also be sensible to ease the tightness of performance targets, repayments schedules, interest rates and the like, in response to overall macro-economic conditions. But there are obvious potential problems with such an approach. If conditionality is to be operated in a truly contra-cyclical fashion this would mean not only easing conditionality in a recession (which could mean that some countries gain too-easy access) but also tightening it in a boom, which might mean that countries could be refused finance on the ground that there is a global excess of liquidity.

4.48 Whether or not such contra-cyclicality of conditionality is workable or desirable, it seems doubtful that IMF conditionality should be varied in a pro-cyclical fashion. Tight performance targets led to the cancellation of IMF arrangements totalling SDR 4.1 billion in 1982, resulting in a significant decline in net IMF loan commitments under standby and extended arrangements — from SDR 12.1 billion in 1981 to SDR 2.4 billion in 1982 — in the midst of a major global recession.

IMF and World Bank Lending for Structural Adjustment

4.49 The external shocks of the last decade have resulted in balance-of-payments problems for which traditional classifications have proved unsuitable. While traditionally there had been a distinction between deficits that were temporary and self-reversing, and those that were due to excess demand and/or exchange rate over-valuation, the major deficits of the 1970s belonged in neither category. The oil shocks were not self-reversing and the resulting deficits were clearly not caused by excess demand. Demand restraint and exchange rate devaluation could not by themselves cure longer-run payments deficits in the absence of investment programmes designed to increase exports and reduce imports; such adjustments necessarily involve a substantial period of time. The need for programmes of structural adjustment was recognised both by the IMF and by the World Bank. The IMF evolved its Extended Fund Facility in 1974, supplemented by multi-year standbys and the Supplementary Financing Facility. The World Bank, for its part, introduced in 1979 its programme of Structural Adjustment Loans (SALs).

4.50 The World Bank's SALs aim to help developing countries re-establish a manageable balance-of-payments position, while maintaining the maximum feasible development effort. SAL funds have been limited by the Bank's rule that not more than 10 per cent of World Bank Group lending should be in programme (or non-project) form; there are now signs that this constraint can be eased.

4.51 SALs carry conditionality, as do IMF loans, although the Bank has sought to develop country programmes on the basis of 'policy dialogue', rather than imposing quantitative performance targets as the IMF does. Even so, SAL conditionality has been criticised as excessive and relying too much on rapid change through wider use of market incentives. Policy dialogue should be encouraged further. The World Bank's articles specify that members' different economic systems must be respected.

4.52 These *ad hoc* Fund and Bank responses to structural adjustment needs have presented developing countries with opportunities for alternative institutional approaches to the same problem. While there is no explicit ruling on this matter, the convention has grown that before a country approaches the World Bank for a SAL it should first have entered into a standby arrangement with the IMF. The emergence of widespread structural deficits and the overlapping interests of the

World Bank and the IMF in dealing with them require that there be consideration of how these two institutions can most effectively contribute to an improved overall response. Obviously, improved Fund/Bank arrangements are called for in EFF/SAL programmes whether or not the adjustment problems originated externally.

4.53 The important distinction between the World Bank as a development agency and the IMF as a provider of short- and medium-term balance-of-payments finance should not be allowed to obscure the fact that policies cannot readily be compartmentalised into those serving the process of adjustment as distinct from those promoting growth. The Fund must be concerned with growth and equity, and the Bank, correspondingly, must concern itself with macro-economic balance. Both the Fund's EFF and the Bank's SAL are appropriate responses to genuine financing needs.

4.54 Countries engaged in structural adjustment should be expected to maintain a dialogue with the lending institutions and to formulate policies for considerably longer periods of time than previously. The EFF approach is therefore an inherently more appropriate response to structural adjustment difficulties than is a series of one-year standby agreements. By the same token, care should be taken to ensure that short-term triggers which in the past would have led to suspension of IMF programmes are not permitted to damage a longer-term programme of adjustment. If formal performance targets are retained they should be reviewed less frequently than quarterly, and be more readily waived as appropriate.

4.55 The design of policies for structural adjustment evolves through a joint process involving the Fund and Bank staffs, irrespective of the particular institutional route originally taken by the country seeking external credit. Joint Fund/Bank missions should be the norm. Fund and Bank staff should also more routinely be assisted by outside experts to lend greater soundness as well as credibility to their views. This could involve, at the very early stages of structural adjustment operations, expert panels like those whose judgements countries have sought to invoke in the past during periods of deadlock with the lending institutions.

4.56 Joint appraisals by the staffs of the Fund and the Bank are necessary if the skills of each institution are to be best deployed in dealing with the common problem where the requirements of adjustment shade into development. A more desirable formal step in dealing with structural adjustment lending is for both institutions to assume, and declare, a joint responsibility for the relevant adjustment programmes. If this is done, countries would be expected to apply simultaneously for an EFF from the Fund and for an SAL from the

Bank; they would then negotiate the structural adjustment programme jointly with both institutions. The division of labour between the two would correspond to that of their traditional skills. The Fund would negotiate the conditions for prudent demand management policies while the Bank would deal with questions of investment priorities over the medium-term, and such issues as fiscal reform and institutional development.

4.57 A further stage of reform might over the longer-term be implemented in the light of experience gathered with the working out of joint programmes of this sort. This reform could involve the merging of the IMF's EFF and the World Bank's SAL facility into a single separate lending entity under the direction of an Executive Board, where representation between developing and industrialised countries would be better balanced and free from weighted voting considerations. The new entity, standing mid-way between the Fund and the Bank, would be in a position to maintain, on a basis of periodic secondment, staff members from each institution whose energies would be specifically addressed to working out the conditions for structural adjustment programmes.

Chapter 5

Commercial Lending and Debt Management

Commercial Bank Finance

5.1   In the 1970s both domestic and international capital flows were increasingly channelled through the commercial banking system. Bond markets and equity flows were inhibited by the high degree of uncertainty that inflation brings, and donor governments, grappling with severe internal problems, have been reluctant to increase external aid.

5.2   According to the BIS, of the aggregate current account deficit of the non-OPEC developing countries between 1973 and mid-1982, fully 45 per cent was covered by net banking inflows. Of the total outstanding non-OPEC developing country medium- and long-term debt of $520 billion at the end of 1982, a third was owed to commercial banks on their own account, compared with 13 per cent in 1971. A further 20 per cent was owed to export credit agencies (but channelled through commercial banks), compared with 27 per cent in 1971. Nine per cent was owed to other private creditors, including bond-holders, and 36 per cent to official lenders.

5.3   Although little of the commercial bank finance was overtly extended as balance-of-payments support, much of it served indirectly as an additional source of liquidity. Reliance on this form of external finance has brought problems for borrowers. Initially, as the international situation deteriorated and as they began to run into balance-of-payments difficulties, some developing countries were able to postpone necessary adjustment through easy access to medium- and long-term international bank loans. However, since such countries continued to run large deficits in the current account of their balance-of-payments, they experienced a deterioration in credit-standing. Longer-term loans then became available only at higher interest rate spreads and there was an increasing tendency for banks to offer credits only for shorter maturities. In some cases, funds dried up altogether as banks reached the limit of their desired exposure. These responses obviously only served to make a bad situation worse.

5.4 Moreover, much commercial bank finance has been made available on variable interest rate terms. Hence borrowing countries have become increasingly vulnerable to fluctuations in the level of international interest rates. In recent years these rates reached new highs in both nominal and real terms; at the same time, the world recession made it increasingly difficult for borrowers to obtain sufficient foreign exchange to service debt at those higher interest rates as well as maintaining import levels. With a large burden of debt that must frequently be rolled-over, a borrower becomes increasingly vulnerable to fluctuations in market confidence, and latterly there has been a withdrawal by banks in the face of debt crises in a number of countries.

5.5 BIS data show that on 30 June 1978, 46 per cent of outstanding commercial bank loans to developing countries were of a maturity of one-year or less; three years later this had risen to 49 per cent. The deterioration is more striking for some countries or country groups. For the Latin American countries the proportion of short-term debt rose from 41 to 46 per cent in the three years, while for the Middle-Eastern countries it rose from 67 to 80 per cent.

5.6 At the same time as there has been a shortening of the average maturity of the debt of developing countries, there has been a marked slowdown in commercial bank lending to them. According to the BIS, bank lending to the non-OPEC developing countries, adjusted to exclude revaluation effects, was halved in 1982 to $20 billion.[1] In the first half of the year, bank lending was $15.4 billion (compared with $12.4 billion in the first half of 1981); but in the second half it plummeted to $4.6 billion (against $27.5 billion in the second half of 1981). This was largely accounted for by a precipitous drop in lending to Latin American countries — from $30.4 billion in 1981 to $12.0 billion in 1982, including only $200 million in the second half of the year. In addition, flows of private direct investment have fallen-off sharply, especially to the Latin American countries, which can only have exacerbated their already serious financing problems.

---

1.   These figures cover only lending by banks in the BIS reporting area and branches of US banks in certain offshore centres. They are net of repayments.

5.7   The developing countries as a group are likely to face a significant 'financing gap', if the situation does not improve. At the end of 1981, the OECD had forecast for 1982 a deficit in the current account of the balance-of-payments of the non-oil developing countries of $70 billion and a surplus of $35 billion for the OPEC countries. In fact both groups of countries recorded deficits, of $66 billion and $4 billion respectively; the OECD has recently forecast deficits of $51 billion and $29 billion respectively for the two groups of countries in 1983, with similar magnitudes likely in 1984. The OECD figures show a drop of 5 per cent in the import volume of non-oil developing countries in 1982 and a forecast further fall of 2 per cent in 1983.

5.8   It is crucial for the international financial system that confidence is restored in the creditworthiness of the major debtor developing countries. This can only be achieved by the reduction of their current account deficits and the rebuilding of reserves. This is a politically delicate as well as technically complex requirement, the success of which rests in most cases on global economic recovery. Somehow debt-servicing capacity must gradually catch up again with debt-servicing requirements. In the meantime, commercial banks must be persuaded at least to maintain their exposure to developing countries; in particular, they must keep open inter-bank credit lines, which are vital for foreign trade.

5.9   A number of schemes have been suggested to relieve commercial banks of some of their existing exposure in developing countries and to lengthen the maturity of the debt of these countries. Their object is to allow the banks to escape from debt-created illiquidity which inhibits their capacity to contribute to overall recovery and to restore the debtor countries' ability to undertake productive new investments. Without such debt restructuring, it is argued, current 'solutions' only pile up more problems for tomorrow.

5.10 These schemes typically provide for the purchase from the commercial banks by some international agency (or agencies) of part of their developing country loan assets. (The financing of the purchase is achieved in various ways.) The agency would then restructure the country's debt on a longer-term, fixed-interest basis; in some versions, repayments would vary with export performance. The developing countries would pay the agency a fee for such restructuring and the banks would contribute by accepting less than the full value of their loans. Banks would not be allowed to exchange all of their exposure to any one country in order to ensure that they maintain an interest in that country and are thus encouraged to continue extending trade credit to it. They would have to be convinced that their potential loss from continuing to hold the developing country's debt would exceed their actual loss from receiving less than full value for it from the agency. In cases where they have significant exposure, banks may prefer to reschedule themselves. This has in the past been a profitable exercise. Banks may perhaps be persuaded to participate if supervisors agreed to accord significantly more relaxed treatment of 'swapped' loans than of rescheduled loans.

5.11 Such schemes run the risk of having the entirely perverse effect of drying-up credit to participating countries. If a commercial bank has got to the stage of admitting it needs to offload a substantial part of its exposure to a particular country, it will probably also have taken the decision not to extend further credit to that country; if not, then such a decision could be forced upon it or upon other potential lenders by frightened depositors. The schemes would therefore have to be universal and perhaps also insist upon continued dealings with the country as a condition of participation. Even then, they run the risk of 'spoiling' the market for credit for years to come.

5.12 While such proposals for large-scale restructuring may have some merit, they do not seem to be practical at the present time. They are still seen as unnecessarily painful to all parties — debtor countries, creditor countries and commercial banks. They could also deflect flows away from poorer countries. For these reasons their possible functioning should be further analysed and they should be kept as contingency plans to be used if the situation at some future stage deteriorates dramatically (see Chapter 8).

5.13 In the longer-term, the maturity profile and use of commercial bank loans to developing countries must be improved. Short-term lending by banks should be used mainly for trade finance. The provision of medium-term cross-border loans by commercial banks is likely to be less easy while the debt problem lasts, and thereafter should not be over-encouraged again. If the money is effectively being used for balance-of-payments purposes, it delays recourse to the IMF, and is difficult to service if a crisis develops. Project lending is more appropriate for banks, but even here the terms need to be watched. Too often such lending represents an uneasy compromise: too long for the banks but too short for the requirements of the project. In some cases this problem can be eased by co-financing with the World Bank or some other multilateral development bank. We revert to this in Chapter 6.

Crisis Management

5.14 Co-ordinated action on the part of major governments, the BIS and the IMF has been effective in the handling of debt crises in Poland, Mexico, Brazil and some other hard-pressed developing countries over the past year and a half. The commercial banks have achieved a degree of co-operation with one another and with official institutions that was hardly conceivable only two years ago. Even so, these crises are still far from fully resolved.

5.15 Whatever the precise mechanisms for the resolution of the current difficulties and dangers in the international financial system, there is an obvious need to devise longer-term and regularised means of reducing the fears and uncertainties that have characterised recent 'crises'. As shown above, these means include improved and internationally co-ordinated contra-cyclical mechanisms and policies; a permanent relative decline in the role of commercial bank finance and relative increase in official multilateral financing arrangements for sovereign borrowers requiring balance-of-payments support; and improved ways to provide timely expansion in international liquidity in keeping with global requirements. Even with such changes, however, there may nevertheless from time to time, and possibly quite soon again, be problems of the kind recently experienced: debt 'crises' and the need for rescheduling; the need for emergency liquidity injections not only for countries but also for commercial banks; and the need for maintaining confidence in the international financial system itself. Since even one 'failure' can have wide ramifications, improved 'back-up' arrangements for possible future crises deserve advance planning. In this section the elements of an improved longer-run system are described. In Chapter 8 contingency plans against the possibly disastrous effects of an aborted global recovery are considered.

Debt Crises and Orderly Rescheduling

5.16 The deterioration in the world economy and the sharp contraction of private lending to East European countries and to developing countries from 1981 onwards has led to a spate of reschedulings. In the 10 months through June 1983 the value of cross-border debt being re-negotiated with commercial banks was over 20 times larger than in any previous year. As many as 40 countries were reported to have agreed to debt reschedulings, or to be seeking a rescheduling of part of their debt or to be in substantial payments arrears. The total outstanding debt of these countries to commercial banks was estimated at around $250 billion in mid-1982. A substantial part of new lending to developing countries has been linked since the end of 1982 to rescheduling agreements. The IMF in fact has made this a condition for its own assistance to some countries with debt problems.

5.17 Although each instance of rescheduling of developing country debt has had unique characteristics by virtue of political and economic differences between countries, certain common patterns have emerged which demonstrate the need to continue to improve arrangements for dealing with debt crises. There have usually been three parties involved on the credit side of debt renegotiations: the IMF, creditor foreign governments and commercial banks. Separate negotiations with each of these are required, and problems of co-ordination have arisen. Commercial banks and sovereign lenders usually require, as a condition of convening a rescheduling meeting, that the debtor country conclude a financial arrangement with the IMF subject to upper tranche conditionality. On the other hand, the Fund needs to know details of foreign exchange availability before it can proceed very far with designing an adjustment programme. Similarly, creditors want to see domestic economic measures being implemented, while the debtor country often wants to know the outcome of the rescheduling before taking action. Commercial banks seek priority with respect to both principal repayments and interest payments, whereas official creditors will not accept a status which is not 'comparable' (however that may be defined) with commercial banks. Also, the interests of banks holding only short-term debt may not be compatible with those of banks with longer-term exposure in the debtor country; and those of banks with only light involvement may not be compatible with those of banks with heavy involvement. In addition, the categories of creditors have different approaches to the rescheduling. Official creditors will generally reschedule both principal and interest payments, as well as related arrears, on medium- and long-term debt, but not payments relating to short-term debt. Commercial banks, however, because of their concern about non-performing assets, have seldom rescheduled interest arrears, and have never rescheduled future interest payments.

5.18 Rescheduling of *official* obligations has been performed for over a quarter of a century by the informal group of the main OECD countries known as the Paris Club. This now consists of officials from the creditor countries and the relevant debtor country, together with representatives of the IMF, the World Bank, the OECD and UNCTAD. The Report has already urged the greater involvement of the World Bank in the design of adjustment programmes (paragraph 4.55). The Bank should also play a more prominent role in debt management and rescheduling. More generally, there should be checks and balances in rescheduling operations to ensure that all parties are fairly treated. It should eventually be possible to develop and adhere to general principles of rescheduling which reduce the present *ad hoc* character of rescheduling and thus avoid charges of inter-country variability of treatment. These requirements might sensibly include the extension of Paris Club agreements to longer periods than the present customary one to two years. The development of such agreed approaches might be furthered by increased consultation among debtors.

5.19 The process of private debt rescheduling could be improved in a number of areas. Above all, improved information and analysis of evolving credit positions could reveal funding difficulties in advance of severe crises and, with debtor-creditor co-operation, encourage partial rescheduling, probably linked to stabilisation programmes in which the IMF and frequently the World Bank are likely to play major roles. Once private rescheduling appears necessary, co-operation not only among private creditors but also between them and the IMF, the World Bank where appropriate, and the central banks of the creditor countries remains desirable.

5.20 Concerted action by creditor banks is vital to the success of rescheduling, particularly in ensuring that short-term credit lines are maintained and that the banks do not reduce the level of longer-term exposure. It may be desirable to consolidate the experience gained thus far in *ad hoc* committees in a semi-permanent organisation, analogous to the official Paris Club. Central banks can contribute by helping to ensure that smaller banks with limited exposure to problem countries do not seek to withdraw funds. They may also seek, to some degree, to harmonise domestic regulations concerning provision for bad and doubtful debts which may impede co-operation between banks in different countries.

Bank Supervision and Lender of Last Resort Arrangements

5.21 In the crisis atmosphere of the past year the commercial banks have been working closely with the IMF, the BIS and individual central banks of major countries in arranging rescheduling agreements for a number of developing and East European countries. In some instances the banks have been pressed by their central banks and the IMF to increase their exposure in particular countries as part of overall financial rescue packages.

5.22 To a considerable extent the difficulties of the banks in recent years were the product of inadequate earlier official acceptance of responsibility for the recycling of OPEC surpluses; possible future bank difficulties in an improved international financial system may be similarly ascribed to official policy inadequacies. At the same time, as within national economies, the implications for the entire financial system of major difficulties among commercial banks are grave enough to warrant official 'intervention' regardless of the apportionment of responsibility for them. The IMF, while in principle at the centre of the multilateral financial system, is merely the creature of its member governments, and still possesses only limited funds for the provision of credit or the development of authority for the imposition of rules for its member governments, let alone for private institutions. Similar limitations exist in the case of BIS activities. BIS assistance and central bank swaps generally can only be of a short-term bridging nature. Such loans must also be secured or have 'the clear promise of Fund or other resources from which the bridging loan can be repaid'. It would seem that for the foreseeable future, the prime responsibility for the health of the commercial banks must continue to rest with national monetary authorities, which are still the only regulators of private financial activities whether domestic or international.

5.23 Since 1975 and the Herstatt Bank failure, the BIS and central banks have sought to improve their monitoring of the international banking system. To move beyond mere monitoring towards increased and/or co-ordinated supervision or regulation runs rapidly into the practical difficulty that every country has its own way of regulating its financial institutions, whether with respect to domestic or international lending. There is at present active debate concerning appropriate credit appraisal techniques, the possible need for tightened official prudential controls and generally increased national regulation for international bank lending. Despite the evident difficulties, efforts should nevertheless continue to achieve greater uniformity and appropriateness of the effects of divergent national practices. More immediately crucial, however, though difficult to separate entirely from the supervision issue, is the provision of adequate 'lender of last resort' (lolr) arrangements for international banks.

5.24 There has been some discussion of commercial bank co-operation to establish a 'safety net' of their own, through the creation of a fund on which they could each draw in the event of liquidity difficulties or through a formal network of inter-bank standby lines. The commercial banks are probably unwilling to commit themselves to pick up the bill for each others' mistakes or imprudent decisions, and competition is likely to limit the degree to which adequate back-up supervisory mechanisms could be agreed, even if such a high degree of bank co-operation were socially desirable, which may itself be a controversial matter. There does seem to be a need for official provision of lolr facilities with respect to international bank activity, a counterpart to the longstanding lolr function offered by national central banks.

5.25 Following the Herstatt case, the BIS central bank governors announced that they were satisfied that 'means are available . . . and will be used if and when necessary' for the provision of temporary liquidity. This is the only official statement on international lolr facilities. Contrary to popular belief, the 1975 Basle Concordat covers the supervisory responsibilities of parent and host authorities for branches and subsidiaries of foreign banks in cases of liquidity or solvency problems but does not specifically cover lolr responsibilities.

The latter are not addressed in the 1983 revision of the Concordat either. Supervisory and lolr responsibilities are, of course, linked. If a problem can be spotted before it develops into a crisis, there will be less need for lolr facilities. However, some banking establishments still escape supervision, especially in the offshore centres. The Concordat's division of responsibilities between parent and host country central bank, although clear in principle, can be unsatisfactory in practice. Host country authorities have primary responsibility for supervising the liquidity of all banks operating within their jurisdiction, including the subsidiaries of foreign banks. Supervision of the solvency of foreign banks remains the responsibility of the authorities in the parent country. This can lead to one central bank having responsibility for liquidity for the subsidiary of a parent bank whose supervisory authority in its country of origin has failed to exercise adequate prudential control over the parent's overseas subsidiaries and branches. The introduction of consolidated reporting has alleviated some fears, but the Banco Ambrosiano case highlights the fact that 'grey' areas remain; and the recent revisions and clarifications of these supervisory responsibilities have not cleared them all away.

5.26 Credible lolr facilities are undoubtedly crucial for the maintenance of confidence. But the establishment of some sort of formal supra-national lolr, however desirable in principle, may be some way off: it would implicitly involve participating central banks relinquishing some of their sovereignty. It would also raise difficult questions of how banks from non-participating countries would be treated and, indeed, some offshore centres have no lolr capacity.

5.27 While efforts to move toward such international facilities continue, immediate steps can be taken. In any major liquidity crisis, individual central banks may quickly exhaust their foreign exchange reserves. Agreements on lines of assistance, for example through currency swaps, in which the US Federal Reserve must play a crucial role, are therefore necessary. Bank supervisors might wish to bolster long-term confidence by making a formal declaration on lolr facilities. In particular, they could announce the formal setting up of new inter-central bank lines of credit, their own further clarification of responsibilities, and commitment to BIS leadership in periods of crisis. However, they may wish, on moral hazard grounds, to avoid giving precise details of how any such lolr agreement would work; banks should not be tempted to be imprudent, or less prudent, in consequence of a belief that assistance will always be forthcoming. It may also be that such announcements would do little for confidence; and that only experience can demonstrate the true effectiveness of international lolr arrangements.

Improved Information

5.28 There can be little doubt that better information will improve the process of credit risk appraisal, and reduce the likelihood of major 'surprises', even though information is by no means the whole story. Although some progress has been made in this area, there is still scope for further development. The provision of reliable and consolidated debt data is still too long delayed, and short-term debt is still particularly inadequately reported. Since short-term debt can accumulate rapidly, both reflecting underlying liquidity problems and itself bringing on the prospect of a crisis, it is crucial that timely information on the size and quality of this type of debt be made available. It is equally crucial that the available information is brought to the attention of those who need to absorb it. Present debt reporting systems can be improved by expanding and speeding up those now existing in the World Bank and the BIS. The commercial banks, through their new Institute of International Finance (IIF)[1], plan to exchange more information among themselves and seek a better exchange with the IMF and the World Bank.

5.29 Improving information does, however, raise some difficult issues, not least those of the confidential status of information obtained by all parties and just how much of it should be exchanged. The IMF and the World Bank are faced with a particularly difficult problem in managing their relations with borrowers on the one hand and with banks on the other, whether in normal times or when playing emergency roles in rescheduling arrangements. Even if the IMF does not insist upon a certain amount of private capital market finance being made available, as it has recently had occasion to do, any IMF programme involves an estimate of private capital account finance which a country is likely to be able to attract. Co-operation between the IMF and the commercial banks is, therefore, very important; but the IMF cannot breach confidentiality in its relationship with the borrowing country. It must be remembered that the IMF and commercial banks have very different roles and motives in their operations in the international capital markets. The IMF's major concern is the overall financial health of member countries and its role is to ensure that a country implements a suitable mix of adjustment and financing to cope with its deficit. Similar considerations motivate the World Bank's Structural Adjustment Lending. The commercial banks, however, are concerned primarily, as profit-making bodies, with responsibility to both shareholders and

---

1. The Institute of International Finance, established in October 1982 by over 30 leading international banks, is situated in Washington. Its aims include the provision of 'a convenient forum through which individual country borrowers can present to lenders information concerning their borrowing needs'. It is hoped that information assembled by the Institute will assist members in their individual lending decisions.

depositors. A divergence of view and of approach to a 'problem country' is therefore quite possible. The IIF may eventually ease the development of this relationship by providing a forum through which the IMF and the World Bank can liaise with the commercial banks as a group.

Chapter 6

Long-term Finance for Development

6.1 Economic progress in the international community depends substantially on the adequacy of international flows of long-term investment capital. The Bretton Woods system acknowledged, particularly, but not only, through the establishment of the World Bank, that an international economic system based on market mechanisms will not automatically provide the flows of long-term international investment funds that are required for global efficiency, nor will it necessarily result in an adequate balance in the distribution of these funds. There are problems associated with risk, uncertainty and information deficiency which reliance on market mechanisms alone will not fully resolve.

6.2 While initially in the post-war period, the immediate international investment problem was seen as one of rehabilitation, the problems of development capital are now paramount. The private capital market, particularly through direct investment flows, has contributed increasingly to meeting growing investment needs. Although not without their own problems, these flows have carried with them technological, entrepreneurial, managerial and marketing skills. Longer-term investment flows of all kinds will have to grow if international development is to proceed at a satisfactory pace. Success in increasing the volume of private long-term finance depends crucially upon the restoration of confidence in the whole system of international finance. Even with progress in this respect, however, systemic problems will remain. Moreover, flows of concessional finance for the poorer countries, which provide some degree of equity in the international system, will have to expand.

6.3   As noted in earlier chapters, the immediate prospects of sustained non-inflationary growth require the maintenance of current credit flows, including commercial bank credit, to countries in debt difficulties. Countries severely hit by recent international events but without the capacity either to attract commercial credit or to adjust without assistance are in particular need of finance.

6.4   For the longer-term, it will be desirable to establish a more appropriate and more stable pattern of international capital flows for development. It seems inevitable that a somewhat smaller, though still important, role will be played by commercial bank lending. For this reason, economic progress in the world as a whole will suffer if there is not a corresponding increase in other flows.

6.5   In a discussion of longer-term financial flows a distinction should be made between middle-income developing countries which can expect to attract commercial finance, and poorer countries which will have to rely on official sources. The relative reduction of commercial bank lending to middle-income developing countries must be made up from other sources. The two most obvious possibilities are bond markets and foreign private direct investment.

Commercial Finance

Improved access for developing countries to bond markets

6.6   The attraction of the international and national bond markets is that they provide fixed interest long-term finance, which is frequently what is required for major development projects. Since the Second World War, however, developing countries have had limited access to the bond markets. In large part, this is because borrowers need to be highly-rated in order to attract investors, who are typically institutions such as pension funds or wealthy trusts and individuals, not nearly as well equipped as commercial banks to undertake the business of risk assessment. Much of the borrowing by developing countries on the bond markets has been in the form of floating rate notes (FRNs) with a variable, and not fixed, interest rate; these are more akin to syndicated bank loans than to traditional bond finance, except that FRNs are negotiable.

6.7   There have been numerous proposals to improve developing countries' access to bond markets. They could, for example, borrow collectively, rather than individually. However, this may involve politically difficult cross-subsidisation between borrowing countries: high-risk countries would benefit from lower-cost finance, but low-risk countries would pay more. It also assumes that lenders would be willing to view the countries as a group, which may be unlikely unless the borrowers are very similar. It has, therefore, been suggested that a fund be established which would provide guarantees or partial guarantees for bond issues, whether national or multinational, by developing countries. There would be many practical problems in setting up such a fund, not least in persuading the industrialised countries to contribute. If the fund were to be self-financing, the developing countries would have to pay a guarantee premium and cheaper finance would not necessarily have been provided.

6.8   Notwithstanding the difficulties involved, all such schemes and further efforts to tap bond markets on behalf of middle-income developing country borrowers deserve further technical exploration and, where appropriate, official support. Where official support, in effect, transfers resources from less creditworthy developing countries to better-off potential borrowers, however, one must pause to consider the opportunity costs. Given the limits to likely official support and the probable slow pace of spontaneous change in the bond markets, most observers are not optimistic about the possibility of a significant surge in developing country borrowing from this source in the 1980s.

Direct investment

6.9   One disadvantage of debt finance is the risk that the income earned on the proceeds of borrowing may fall below the cost of servicing it. This risk is increased when debt is contracted at floating or variable interest rates. By contrast, the yield on equity finance is related to the success of the particular venture. Such finance is therefore appropriate to large development projects. The risk assumed by deficit countries on their external liabilities has increased in recent years, not only through the rapid increase in those liabilities, but also because a growing proportion of them has taken the form of commercial bank debt.

6.10 While foreign private direct investment (FPDI) has been increasing in developing countries and is frequently now provided in less packaged and more flexible and attractive ways, the rapid expansion of commercial bank finance has reduced its relative role in capital flows. An increase in FPDI is needed not only to boost the total flow of development finance but also to improve its quality. It is important that there should be a better relationship, than typically there was in the late 1970s, between gestation periods and profitability of projects on the one hand and the terms and conditions under which capital is provided on the other. Difficulties in securing increases in other forms of long-term capital, for example multilateral development bank lending and bond issues, together with other advantages of FPDI, including its association with technology, management, marketing skills and market access, strengthen the case for increased emphasis on such investment.

6.11 FPDI is influenced critically by the global economic climate, economic and political conditions and prospects in the host country, and the latter's policies towards transnational corporations (TNCs). A sustained recovery in economic growth and trade, lower interest rates and a rolling-back of protectionist barriers in the industrialised countries would do much to increase interest in investing in the development of raw materials, commodity processing and manufacturing in the developing countries.

6.12 There are a number of initiatives that could be taken in the near-term to improve the international investment climate. The flow of FPDI has been impeded by what are perceived as significant constraints by both parties. Governments of developing countries have, in general, been wary of the market power and financial strength of TNCs, some of which have a turnover greater than the total GDP of many small countries. They have been fearful that foreign-owned firms will expand to the detriment of indigenous enterprises; that they will deprive the country of natural and human resources and through the remittance of profits abroad will exacerbate balance-of-payments difficulties. There are also political fears of foreign domination or interference which tend to reinforce economic fears of exploitation. The effect of these perceptions in host countries has been an ambivalent attitude towards FPDI which, in turn, has engendered TNC fears of expropriation, control of profit repatriation, etc.

6.13 Fortunately, there has been some improvement in the relations between TNCs and host countries in recent times. The tendency towards the 'unbundling' of the investment package has enabled developing countries to be more selective in the form in which foreign participation is accepted. This, together with the greater ability of developing countries to undertake joint ventures, a greater role taken by facilitating agencies such as the International Finance Corporation, investment insurance arrangements, settlement in principle of the natural resources sovereignty issue, and greater attention to the rules of the game, have all helped.

6.14 But much more needs to be done. Negotiations should be completed to establish effective codes of conduct on the activities of TNCs and on the transfer of technology in relation to their operations in developing countries; and investment insurance arrangements should be extended and improved.

6.15 All the major industrialised countries have established national investment guarantee schemes covering non-commercial risk. These schemes have limitations, however. They only apply to those developing countries with which bilateral investment protection agreements have been concluded. Also, some schemes are very limited in their coverage and do not yet inspire great confidence. These schemes need further improvement and the limited existing private investment insurance arrangements could perhaps expand. However, these developments would not remove all the gaps and weaknesses which at present exist. Some national schemes, especially those in the smaller industrialised countries, are inhibited by inadequate risk diversification and these schemes do not make adequate provision for ventures involving more than one home country. Some capital surplus countries, for example certain OPEC members, still do not have national schemes. Regional schemes could help but efforts in this direction are still very limited geographically as well as in terms of coverage. The World Bank is considering the establishment of a multilateral agency for the insurance of political risk, and this should be encouraged.

6.16 Bilateral investment treaties between pairs of industrialised and developing countries have much to commend them, since, in principle, they can create the right psychological atmosphere for flows of risk capital from the former to the latter type of country. However, care should be taken to promote equity in the relationship, perhaps even involving non-reciprocity in certain crucial aspects.

6.17 The mechanisms for the settlement of disputes in agreements relating to investment commonly fall short of what is needed. Bilateral investment agreements between home and host governments aim to secure protection against discriminatory legal and administrative action. However, they do not usually provide mechanisms whereby a host government and foreign investor can directly settle any dispute arising between them in relation to the treaty. The International Centre for the Settlement of Investment Disputes (ICSID) was established under the auspices of the World Bank to fill this gap. Few cases, however, have been referred to it and its effectiveness has been limited by the non-participation of many developing countries, including those which believe that disputes within their boundaries should be settled under their national jurisdiction. Nonetheless, a growing number of investment agreements do include provision to submit future disputes to ICSID and many host countries have adopted legislation accepting its jurisdiction. This trend could be encouraged.

6.18 Finally, as suggested below, further increases in the capital of the International Finance Corporation would enable the IFC not only to expand its lending and equity investment activities but, through its catalytic role, to increase participation by local and foreign investors.

6.19 All of these suggestions should help to increase the flow of FPDI. In addition, they should assist in diversifying the direction of such flows, which are highly concentrated in the industrialised countries and the more economically advanced developing nations. Better risk insurance and improved relations and understanding could see more investment directed at the potential in lower- and middle-income countries.

New financial instruments

6.20 The experience with commercial bank borrowing has generated new interest not only in longer maturities (bond finance) but also in increased risk-sharing via equity and equity-type forms of finance. Equity finance may be obtained, at least to some degree, without resort to the complete FPDI package. Portfolio investors in equity may be more effectively sought out by developing country borrowers. Efforts to construct new equity-type financial instruments should be encouraged, for example an instrument combining both equity and loan features — what is sometimes referred to as 'quasi-capital'. One form of this is a 'conditional loan' made by a national or international financing institution, under which the loan debt-service would be paid, particularly in the initial years, only if the project generated sufficient income. Another innovative instrument protects foreign equity investors against exchange risk by denominating their finance in dollars instead of in local currency. The World Bank Group, and in particular the IFC, can be an important initiator of ideas in this sphere.

Official Export Credit

6.21 Export credit provides an additional source of finance for developing countries which is important at this time of tight access to external capital. As short-term finance it is also an appropriate form of financing for commercial banks. Export finance, including supplier credit, may increasingly involve official loans and guarantees. Some of this finance has longer maturities and subsidised interest rates which gives it advantages over finance provided by commercial banks on market terms. The issue is not straightforward, however, since such credits are always tied and the costs of the goods supplied may in practice be above those from other sources. More generally, such measures can encourage bilateralism in international trade, and often, where they do not reflect the real costs of credit, serve as a trade protection measure for the lending country. The provision of export credit on normal market terms is a desirable adjunct to exporting, and developing countries looking to expand export markets should be encouraged to consider such arrangements, particularly if they can tap external sources of finance to do so. Where it is subsidised, however, countries unable to provide similar financial subsidies are disadvantaged. Every effort must be made therefore to reduce the distorting effects of tied and subsidised export and supplier credits. Under the OECD Arrangement on Guidelines for Officially Supported Export Credits (the so-called 'Consensus'), the industrialised countries are endeavouring to limit competition among export suppliers by fixing the price of export credit. As with other stabilising arrangements, this problem would be better dealt with on a multilateral basis involving consumers as well as suppliers; further international attention to this problem is needed. In the absence of rules, new 'trade wars' in banking services may complicate the still tenuous and partial intergovernmental agreements in the sphere of export credit. In this connection governmental agreements to limit intervention in overseas commercial bank lending may well be relevant.

Multilateral Development Banks

6.22 Multilateral development banks (MDBs), including their soft-loan funds, are an extremely important and distinct source of long-term finance for developing countries. During 1975-82 they accounted for 12 per cent of total net disbursements to developing countries from all sources. Apart from their many well known qualitative advantages in terms of project design and administrative procedures, they have been particularly responsive to the needs of low-income countries and have provided funds for sectors and purposes not amenable to financing from other sources. In addition, they have often acted as a catalyst for resources from other sources, including private markets. While the balance between these two separate functions — provision of finance from own resources and mobilising other resources — changes from time to time, there is a continuing need for both.

6.23 In the immediate future, because of the enlarged and urgent needs of many countries, particularly low-income ones, and also because of increasing constraints on expanding other flows, one of the most important tasks must be to increase the lending programmes of the MDBs. This is particularly essential for the World Bank Group which is by far the largest source of multilateral long-term finance for developing countries, accounting for about 40 per cent of such flows.

6.24 The argument for expanding the flow of long-term finance through the MDBs, and particularly the World Bank, deserves spelling out in some detail. It rests upon the twin facts of the manifest firm demand for long-term capital capable of yielding a high real rate of return, and the limited willingness or capacity of commercial banks, bond markets or foreign investors to supply it. The World Bank was expressly created to overcome such examples of imperfection in global capital markets. Its record of overall cost-effectiveness in that role is nowhere seriously questioned.

6.25 It is obviously not possible precisely to quantify the developing countries' demand for long-term finance or the rates of return that can be earned on it. But there does not at present appear to be any shortage of fundable development projects. Even in those countries that have recently completed major infrastructure projects, more complex demands are emerging — for the development of food production, for new manufacturing industries, for the development of export activities, for structural adjustment programmes, etc. The examples of North America and Australia in the nineteenth century and, more recently, those of such countries as India, Malaysia and South Korea indicate the probability of continuing capacity to employ development capital in highly productive ways over long periods of time.

6.26 Private capital can and should be encouraged to supply more development finance. But there are limits to what can be expected from these long-term sources and it has proved dangerous to rely upon short- and medium-term funds for this purpose. Private and official sources of finance should not therefore be seen as alternatives. Expanded MDB activity is likely to encourage increased private capital flows to developing countries, both by direct complementary project financing and by helping to create or maintain a favourable environment for the continuing process of orderly growth and development.

6.27 To increase lending programmes requires additional resources for the MDBs. At present, they face serious problems in securing such increases. Most depend heavily on borrowings in capital markets to finance their lending programmes but they also need adequate capital subscribed by governments to provide a capital base and guarantee for borrowed funds, especially as they operate on extremely conservative gearing ratios. In particular, the soft-loan windows of the MDBs, which are totally dependent on periodic replenishments and annual appropriations in donor countries, are vulnerable to the deteriorating aid climate.

The World Bank

6.28 When the last capital increase for the World Bank (IBRD)[1] was being negotiated, discussion centred around achieving a real growth in Bank lending over the first half of the 1980s of 5-7 per cent per annum.

---

1. The World Bank Group comprises the IBRD, IDA and IFC. This section deals with the IBRD; subsequent sections deal with IDA and IFC. See also Appendix I.

A consensus was achieved on a nominal growth of 12 per cent per annum. With inflation rates higher than originally expected, real growth in Bank lending could not reach anticipated rates. At the same time new demands were placed upon World Bank financing — urgent pressures for energy development, the accession to membership of the People's Republic of China, and the requirements of adjustment to severely deteriorated terms of trade. In the short- to medium-run future, there is a further need for expanded World Bank activity in the light of cutbacks in commercial bank lending and the need to restore orderly and balanced global economic recovery.

6.29 For purposes of discussion, it is best to distinguish the activities of the World Bank proper, together with the 'hard' lending of the regional and sub-regional development banks, from those of IDA and the analogous smaller soft-loan windows of other MDBs. (Multilateral concessional lending is discussed later also, in the section on official development assistance.)

6.30 The World Bank must continue to play its critical present role in developing country finance. Following the agreement to double its capital in fiscal year 1980, the World Bank is operating a $60 billion lending programme for 1982-86. In spite of the greatly enlarged demands on its resources, it has not yet been possible to raise *commitments* above previously agreed levels. Unless plans are changed, commitments in real terms will stagnate or even decline in the years ahead. The new Special Action Programme aims to accelerate *disbursements* temporarily by such means as relaxing previous limits on structural adjustment lending, expanding sectoral lending and other non-project finance, and financing a greater share of project costs; but the total commitments remain largely unaffected. The acceleration of disbursements and the expansion of non-project lending are especially welcome in the present circumstances. A significant further increase in overall commitments is nevertheless essential to maintain the momentum of increased disbursements. The Special Action Programme in any case is intended only for World Bank clients; IDA — desperately short of funds — has no equivalent.

6.31 The Bank's lending programme is being held back not because of any immediate prospect of breaching the statutory lending limits or because of any resource constraints, but from concern that an increase from the planned levels would generate pressures on government budgets for an early further capital increase. Such a pre-emptive approach seems to be wholly unjustified. The Bank is constrained from expanding its lending activities by the combination of its limited capital base, its capital-lending ratio (a very conservative one-to-one) and its cautious policy of remaining within its 'sustainable lending limit'.[1] An easing of these constraints would allow the Bank to respond to widely perceived needs. Changes in the capital-lending ratio do not at present seem likely because of the difficulty of amending the Bank's Articles of Agreement and the management's concern that faith not be broken with current holders of World Bank bonds. It is therefore all the more important that early steps are taken to increase the Bank's capital. Meanwhile, as the capital increase is planned, there should be no reason to limit the Bank's lending by the additional consideration of the sustainable level of lending.

6.32 There is a precedent for the World Bank to follow IMF quota expansions with its own capital increases. In present circumstances a selective capital increase of about $20 billion would parallel the eighth quota increase. Such an increase need not impose demands upon national budgets for several years, but early agreement is required to enable the Bank to attain a 5 per cent per annum increase in its commitments by the mid-1980s, in line with the management's recent proposals. In this respect, the decision at UNCTAD VI to invite governments to 'consider constructively' these proposals is to be welcomed. World Bank capital would need to be expanded again after the mid-1980s to enable the Bank to continue to increase its lending.

The International Development Association

6.33 IDA, the soft loan arm of the World Bank Group, is the major source of multilateral aid to developing countries and as such it makes a substantial contribution to the depoliticisation of official development assistance. In 1980, about 80 per cent of its net disbursements went to countries with per capita incomes of less than $410. This compares with 34 per cent for bilateral programmes. Without IDA's activities in these countries the World Bank Group would be unable to claim a 'world' responsibility. Recently, there has been increased involvement of developing countries as IDA donors, and around a third of the donors in the Sixth Replenishment are developing countries. IDA has a good record in the quality of the projects it has financed, and a recent sample survey of completed projects indicated an average rate of return of 18 per cent. A large proportion of its resources go to key sectors such as agriculture and to other projects that directly benefit the poorer sections of the population.

---

1. Under the Bank's Articles, disbursements cannot exceed capital plus reserves. The 'sustainable lending limit' is that level of commitments that can be sustained indefinitely without requiring another capital increase. The limit varies and can be exceeded temporarily, but the commitment rate must then be reduced, without abrupt changes, so that subsequent disbursements do not exceed capital plus reserves.

6.34 In spite of these favourable features, which are widely recognised, and the key position it holds in improving the overall contribution of aid to economic development, IDA is facing a crisis in securing resources and a great threat to its whole future. And this is happening at a time when the oil-importing low-income countries have an enormous need for concessional transfers to alleviate serious balance-of-payments problems caused by circumstances largely outside their control. The problems facing IDA epitomise the critical situation facing international economic co-operation.

6.35 The fate of the $12 billion Sixth Replenishment, once due for completion in June 1983 and now stretched until June 1984, depends critically upon the approval of the US Congress. Beyond that, the negotiations for the Seventh Replenishment need to make speedy progress if it is to commence in July 1984. An IDA VII of $15 billion is required just to maintain its operations in real terms; but more than this amount is needed if IDA is to expand to meet new and enlarged needs arising from the serious structural adjustment problems in the poorer countries, including urgent demands for food and energy production, and from the large increase in the population it must serve following the accession to membership of China.

6.36 The future of IDA depends critically on the United States. Not only is the United States the largest contributor but because of the system of *pro rata* contributions, total replenishment levels are sensitive to its contribution. The willingness of other donors to detach their contributions from the reduced levels of annual US contributions to IDA VI greatly assisted in preventing a sharp reduction of IDA lending. However this special effort relating to temporary crisis circumstances cannot be counted upon in relation to a new replenishment. It is extremely important that all efforts are made to encourage a more positive attitude to IDA, especially by major donors. The United States is proposing a substantial reduction in its contribution. However, it is not the only major country whose action poses a threat to the size of IDA VII. It is vital that all donors play their part in helping to ensure an expanding IDA.

6.37 After its first replenishment, all subsequent IDA replenishments have been at increased levels in real terms. Providing for a 5 per cent real increase over IDA VI disbursements would require a Seventh Replenishment of about $16 billion. However this would still not mean an increase in funds for IDA's traditional recipients if China's needs are to be covered as well. The World Bank staff calculated that an additional $5-6 billion would be necessary (i.e. an IDA VII of around $22 billion) if China's membership and the expanded needs of energy development and structural adjustment in the poorer countries were to be accommodated.

6.38 In the light of current difficulties, proposals are being put forward for the graduation from IDA of some borrowers. While graduation is to be expected as per capita incomes increase beyond traditional IDA limits, eligibility should continue to be based on poverty levels and should not include, as some suggest, 'creditworthiness' which is less tangible, more uncertain and could be more subjective.

6.39 It is vitally important to achieve the full completion by the United States of its IDA VI contribution in 1983/84 and the early completion of negotiations for IDA VII to allow it to start promptly with a commitment authority in 1984/85 at levels which would enable low-income countries to secure real increases in the flow of IDA resources to them. In the future, apart from the real increases which are likely to be required, IDA replenishment should extend for longer periods than three years so as to reduce uncertainties and facilitate orderly investment planning.

Co-financing

6.40 Co-financing between official lenders already takes place and should be encouraged. Co-financing in which the World Bank or other MDBs take the longer maturities (say, those exceeding eight years) and commercial banks take the shorter ones is relatively new.The new co-financing initiatives by the World Bank which could at least help to maintain commercial flows at a time of increased restraint on the part of commercial banks are to be welcomed. In principle this is an area in which progress can and should be made, and there has been much discussion of it in recent months.

6.41 The full impact of co-financing is difficult to measure. Although commercial bank participation in co-financed loans with the World Bank has increased rapidly since 1979, it remains small. Detractors claim that it generates no additional finance. But it does provide the opportunity for second and third tier banks to 'get to know' a new borrower, which may lead to a proper banking relationship being developed and the procurement of profitable ancillary business. The involvement of the World Bank gives lenders the assurance that loan proceeds are being used for priority investment purposes, and the commercial banks benefit from the Bank's considerable expertise at project appraisal. This should lead to a reduction in perceived risk, which for the country may manifest itself in a slightly lower spread. In any case, individual countries may find the possibility of co-financing between the World Bank and commercial banks helpful in their particular circumstances.

6.42 The instruments recently introduced by the World Bank on a trial basis to increase the attractiveness of co-financing to commercial banks, provided they do not become the pre-conditions for normal World Bank lending, could well prove attractive to both borrowers and commercial lenders. Only time will tell whether the Bank has done enough to encourage increased participation by the commercial banks. Undoubtedly the banks would prefer a more concrete link between themselves and the World Bank in cases of payments difficulties, but they may be willing to be more active in view of the possibility of the slight reduction in risk offered by World Bank involvement.

The International Finance Corporation

6.43 The IFC, the third member of the World Bank Group, could play an important and expanding role in the overall effort to secure more private long-term and equity capital for development. With considerable experience and an increased geographic spread to its activities, it is now well placed to promote private investment in a wide range of developing countries. Its efforts to develop investment opportunities, bring partners together, find new sources of equity capital and develop new financial arrangements deserve every support. It should be encouraged to continue to innovate and take risks as it pursues its catalytic objectives. In view of the IFC's potential importance to the current search for more appropriate forms of long-term finance and the fact of its expanding activity, consideration should be given to advancing the date of its next capital increase so as to permit new contributions to resume in 1985. (Its last capital increase was approved in 1977 and subscriptions have only recently been completed.)

Regional and sub-regional development banks

6.44 All the regional development banks (African, Asian, Inter-American) and the sub-regional ones (e.g. Caribbean, East African, etc.), though established in response to particular local circumstances, are essentially based on the World Bank model; they are at present subject to similar strains and financial constraints as the World Bank itself. In any general review of the international economic institutions, the relative roles of the World Bank and the regional and sub-regional banks should be analysed. The latter enjoy certain advantages over the World Bank: they have a greater knowledge of their respective areas and the developing countries themselves play a relatively larger role in their operations and decision-making. Sub-regional banks are often also active in the promotion of economic integration and co-operation. As a long-term strategy, it would be to the general advantage, in terms of both efficiency and politics, if a considered division of functions were worked out. The World Bank might concentrate, for instance, on overall country/adjustment programmes and on larger projects while the regional and sub-regional banks take over responsibility for a greater proportion of more normal MDB-funded projects in their respective areas. The World Bank should, in any case, consider expanding its support for the regional and sub-regional banks, including channelling more funds for project lending through these institutions and, if required, assisting them in their approaches to capital markets. As it does so, it should leave the smaller development banks free to apply their own policies, procedures, terms and conditions in any onlending to their own borrowing member countries; it would be inappropriate for the bigger development banks to use the regional or sub-regional banks as mere agents rather than respecting their independence and identity.

6.45 One particular area of financing, in addition to the usual programme and project loans, to which both the regional and sub-regional banks might wish to give increasing attention, is the provision of funds for financing regional and sub-regional payments arrangements, in order to ease the foreign exchange constraints to the maintenance and expansion of intra-regional and intra-sub-regional trade. Regional and sub-regional projects should also be increasingly encouraged, as might be the re-financing or guaranteeing of credits to finance exports to other countries, regionally or otherwise. The playing of a lead role in the co-ordination of aid from all major bilateral and multilateral donors is also an activity which should be expected from regional and sub-regional development banks. IFC-types of equity and loan investments in the private sector are another activity which deserve more emphasis at the regional and sub-regional level of development banking.

Role of multilateral development banks

6.46 The MDBs, and the World Bank Group in particular, have proven records in facilitating long-term capital flows to developing countries for productive utilisation. At a time when there is a clear and widely agreed need to achieve longer maturities for developing country borrowing, both immediately and for the longer-run, the World Bank's role is particularly important. In the light of the reservations being expressed by some of the Bank's major shareholders about its future role, it is important that there be a general reaffirmation in a 'new Bretton Woods', or even earlier, of its important place, indeed that of all the MDBs, in the international financial scene. It is vital that their activities continue to expand, and that their comparative advantage — in project development, the formulation of overall development programmes, and technical assistance in a variety of areas — be built upon.

Official Development Assistance

6.47 However great may be the role of long-term finance on commercial or near-commercial terms, there will continue to be need for concessional finance. Official development assistance (ODA) is frequently motivated by strategic, political or commercial considerations. There are also often humanitarian considerations. However the principal rationale in terms of overall systemic need lies in the contribution ODA makes to longer-run global welfare in terms of resource and skill development, reduced population growth, and systemic stability. That is not to say that concessional finance does not frequently yield a high rate of return in more conventional economic terms.

6.48 ODA at present occupies an important place in the structure of financial flows to developing countries. While its relative importance in total receipts of external finance dropped markedly from the 1970s — from 42.5 per cent in 1970 to 33.8 per cent in 1981 — its role in particular countries remains crucial. ODA finances about two-thirds of the deficits of the low-income countries and about one-quarter of their investment. For the UN category of Least Developed Countries these contributions are higher still, with ODA providing over three-quarters of the investment in many of them.

6.49 The need for ODA has been heightened in recent years because of the very inadequate provision made for low-income countries in existing mechanisms for expanding international liquidity, and the failure effectively to stabilise commodity prices or earnings. Current circumstances demonstrate the vulnerability of an even wider group of developing countries to severe external shocks and suggest a greater than usual immediate need for development assistance.

6.50 Apart from the poorer countries (located mainly in sub-Saharan Africa and South Asia), there are some twenty-odd mini-states (with populations of less than half a million) in the Caribbean Sea, the Indian Ocean and the Pacific Ocean which, even when their per capita incomes are somewhat higher than those in the poorest countries, face distinct disadvantages in pursuing their development efforts: extremely small domestic markets, a highly concentrated structure of production and exports, lack of 'critical mass' in terms of skills and institutions, and economies that are very vulnerable, fragile, and lacking in resilience in the face of external shocks, including natural disasters. These countries will for a long time also have a great need for external aid on highly concessional terms. However, their combined needs are very small — in fact they constitute only a minimal proportion of global requirements for such resources.

6.51 After an unfortunate drop in 1981, total ODA flows from OECD countries rose again in real terms in 1982. But ODA has not been increasing significantly as a proportion of the GNP of donor countries. The OECD members' ODA is still, on average, only slightly over half (0.39 per cent) of the 0.7 per cent of GNP target which was adopted by the UN in 1970; moreover, OPEC members' ODA, which is about one-fifth of total ODA and over 1 per cent of the GNP of OPEC countries, is on the decline, following the sharp reduction in OPEC surpluses. About one-third of OECD members' ODA is provided through multilateral agencies but, as the current replenishment problems facing IDA, UNDP and IFAD demonstrate, multilateral aid is now looked upon less favourably by donor countries and has recently suffered a relative decline.

6.52 In view of the severe development and adjustment problems facing the low-income countries and their inadequate access to, and inability to use, non-concessional flows, the need to increase concessional flows to them is urgent. But such flows are facing a squeeze not only because of budgetary considerations but also because of the adverse effects on aid distribution arising from the increased importance being attached to strategic and commercial considerations in major donors' aid allocations. The cost to budgets of the present levels of aid is, in relative terms, low. Those donor countries that have not yet written-off earlier official debt owed by the poorest countries ought now at last to do so. Greater recognition of the severity of the problems facing many developing countries could still generate the will and determination for an appropriate response.

6.53 While almost no progress is being made in advancing to the ODA target of 0.7 per cent of GNP, which is still untranslated by some donors into time-specific terms, the industrialised countries which have not yet reached the target did agree at UNCTAD VI to 'redouble their efforts to that end'. Aid targets still serve as a useful benchmark and could be refined so as to encourage increased provision and improved distribution. An overdue area for improvement is in the definition of ODA, long measured as a collection of grants and loans of varying characteristics. Targets for aid should be measured in terms of an internationally standardised method of calculating its 'grant element'. Consideration should be given to ways in which the 0.7 per cent target, redefined as grant element, could be realised as early as possible and in any case not later than the end of the present decade. Progress might be sought via phasing, in which donors agreed to expand commitments according to their capacity to do so, for example by setting aside a given percentage of any annual increase in GNP. A reasonable level for the amount so committed might be 2 to 4 per cent, varying according to a donor's present position in relation to the target. This would be sufficient for OECD countries to achieve the 0.7 per cent target, under current definitions, in four years if their GNP were to grow by 3 per cent a year.

6.54 The aid target might be further refined so as to take account of donors' varying capacities to provide concessional funds. In this context, it is worth recalling that the 0.7 per cent target was agreed only as a minimum. Whilst it is generally recognised that aid distribution should be related to income level, little serious consideration has been given to the application of this principle to the provision of aid, by fixing donors' aid targets on a progressive scale according to per capita income. Such a system would involve all countries, except the very poorest, in the aid effort and could have greater potential for exerting influence on donors currently lagging behind in their commitments.

6.55 Some progress was made in improving targetry by the agreement by most donor countries at the UN Conference on the Least Developed Countries in 1981 to accept a target of 0.15 per cent of GNP or a doubling of aid by 1985 for this group of countries (which now number 36). Since that Conference their economic situation has worsened and it becomes even more vital that the commitment, which has been reaffirmed at UNCTAD VI, is honoured.

6.56 However, current trends do not hold out hope for significant progress in improving the distribution of aid. The proportion of bilateral aid going to low-income countries has declined significantly over the past two decades. Much greater aid per capita goes to middle-income countries. The situation could worsen noticeably if the current relative decline in multilateral aid is allowed to continue, as could well happen if adequate IDA replenishment runs into difficulties. In paragraphs 3.62 and 4.31 suggestions have been made for some increases in aid flows to the poorest countries through specific multilateral channels. The suggestions reflect the need for improved aid distribution and the advantages of multilateral over bilateral aid.

6.57 The relative freedom of multilateral aid from bilateral political and commercial objectives allows it to be more efficiently provided, through international competitive bidding, and to be directed more effectively at areas of need — both geographic and sectoral. As has been shown (paragraph 6.33), a much higher proportion of IDA net disbursements has gone to low-income countries than is the case with bilateral programmes. IFAD also directs its resources for agricultural development particularly to the poor, and it too has been forced to cut its programmes — in consequence of delays and uncertainties concerning donor contributions. These trends must be reversed.

6.58 The relative decline in the multilateral provision of aid is also affecting the further development of multilateral technical co-operation and is endangering the future of the UNDP. The UNDP represents a rationalised approach to the provision of multilateral technical co-operation incorporating flexible and decentralised operations, and supportive of the related technical assistance of other organisations and institutions, including those providing capital assistance. Its multilateral operations and its independence of the international financial institutions have proved advantageous in the provision of independent technical advice and assistance to the developing countries. But its work is being adversely affected by a new shortage of funds and the tendency of major donor countries to give greater relative emphasis to their own bilateral programmes. In technical co-operation, as in finance, a renewed commitment to proven multilateral approaches is called for.

6.59 There are other changes that could improve the impact of existing aid flows. The recession has increased pressures for tying and other conditionality applying to bilateral ODA. Aid is more effective when the recipient is given the choice to purchase in the most favourable market, including other developing countries. However, to reverse the trend towards aid commercialisation would require joint action by donors, since none would wish its funds to be used to the advantage of competitors. Also, in existing circumstances of severe financing constraints in developing countries, the flexibility and quick disbursal of funds provided by non-project, bilateral aid may be particularly helpful. The advantages of a better balance between programme and project aid are publicly recognised by donors, yet little corrective action has been taken and bilateral non-project aid actually declined over the 1970s.

6.60 It would be highly desirable for the balance between programme and project aid to be varied appropriately over the cycle. Low-income countries and a number of island and other smaller economies would benefit particularly from increased programme aid at the present time. The external shocks of recent years have dealt them especially severe blows and, in the absence of adequate offsetting finance, they have been forced into savage compression of import volumes — to the point where reduced imports of materials, spare parts and equipment are unnecessarily setting back not only current incomes but also longer-term development prospects.

6.61 The current inadequacy of available financing facilities comes at a time when under pressure of events many of these countries have made brave attempts to move towards policy frameworks, including exchange rate and budgetary reforms, that are likely to be more supportive of their longer-term development. Unless such adjustment efforts are supported by amounts of concessional and quick-disbursing finance which, in the current circumstances (created in part by the inadequacy of the Sixth Replenishment of IDA), can only become available through additional bilateral ODA, they are doomed to failure. The decisions at the Williamsburg Summit to give 'special attention' to the flow of resources, in particular ODA, to poorer countries is very welcome.

6.62 The case for additional quick-disbursing finance, beyond the amounts presently earmarked, for poor countries during the next two years is overwhelming. Most commendable in this context is a proposal put to UNCTAD by the Netherlands Government. This urges a co-ordinated special donor action programme for the poorer countries, to be implemented through the medium of an *ad hoc* group of bilateral and multilateral donors, and organised by the OECD's Development Assistance Committee (DAC) on the basis of information provided by the World Bank and the IMF. It envisages the raising of additional amounts in the range of $2-4 billion over a period of two years, to be revised as consultations proceed within the *ad hoc* group. This proposal should be sympathetically considered if IDA funds remain inadequate; in fact, if IDA funds were adequate there might have been no need for such a proposal.

6.63 There are some 40 active donors dealing with over 120 developing countries; the scope for duplication, confusion and waste is considerable. Simplification and standardisation of aid procedures, co-ordination of missions, improved consultation as regards projects and objectives, would all ease the burden imposed upon administrations, particularly of the smaller and poorer developing countries. In the case of these countries it is at the same time important that external assistance be offered in such a way as not to prejudice the national autonomy of the recipient or its capacity to develop its own management resources.

6.64 The need for improved arrangements for the multilateral discussion of aid issues is also evident. The Development Committee of the IMF and World Bank has not proved to be effective; OECD's DAC is limited to donor countries; in UN forums, donors decline to take resolutions seriously; the World Bank and regional- or country-specific aid groups and consortia are doing very useful work but their concerns are, by their very nature, geographically limited; and special conferences give rise to vague communiques and easily avoided commitments. There is no authoritative multilateral aid forum, meeting on a regular basis. The publication of the annual DAC report on aid performance and procedures might offer the basis for a joint donor-recipient forum on aid questions, of the kind that is now necessary.

6.65 For the longer term, the objective should be to put aid on a more predictable and assured basis. This will require greater use of forward commitments and longer replenishment cycles, especially where these are still on a very short-term basis, for example one-year at a time in the case of the UNDP. A higher degree of automaticity of provision of funds for multilateral aid should generally be sought. What is required is the gradual evolution of a system of global revenue collection. This revenue could be used initially in the service of pressing global problems such as the protection of the environment and the securing of adequate welfare for all children. It might initially be provided by specific graduated levies, for example on sea-bed resources, and evolve in the long run towards other forms of global revenue raising.

Chapter 7

An Effective and Integrated Regime for International Trade

7.1 Malfunction in the international trading system and inadequate co-ordination between trade and financial policies have contributed significantly to the present global economic difficulties. Even after international economic recovery begins, high levels of unemployment in the industrialised countries will remain for a considerable period. Protectionist sentiment in those countries is still increasing and, while resort to increased protection seems now somewhat restrained, the risk remains that resurgent protectionism will eventually arrest recovery or even precipitate further decline. Agricultural export subsidy 'wars' between the United States and the EEC from time to time threaten the international trading order. Countries heavily dependent on imports for food, energy and raw material supplies, still have reason to fear that new barriers to their manufactured exports will put at risk their economic and political security. Particularly if recovery is slow or aborted, the danger clearly persists of a tragic slide into beggar-my-neighbour protectionism and trade 'wars'. Improved functioning of the trading system is consequently a major element in the prospect for a vigorous and sustained recovery and for greater stability and progress in world development.

Evolution of the Trading System

7.2 The international trading system that emerged in the early post-war years was to be a universal system based on a few key principles and approaches: multilateralism; non-discrimination; openness or transparency; and liberalisation through negotiation on the basis of reciprocity. Behind these were further presumptions that national governments would pursue policies of full employment and domestic stability, and that balance-of-payments equilibrium would be achieved by way of more or less fixed exchange rates.

7.3   The liberalising of trade was based, intellectually, on the free trade argument which put the case that through international co-operation and exchange the world was made more prosperous. Reciprocity in liberalisation is not necessarily equitable. Nor was it a requirement of the intellectual argument, since unilateral liberalisation is itself seen as beneficial. But it nevertheless contributed to expectations of balance in international payments. The unconditional application of liberalising measures to all members gave force to the important non-discrimination principle. It was recognised, as well, that the global benefits would only emerge with a collective adherence to rules and that this would only occur if there existed some means of enforcing them.

7.4   As already stated, the trading arrangements accepted in the late 1940s in the GATT had various gaps: they failed to deal effectively with agricultural trade, for which substantial exceptions or qualifications to the rules were provided, reflecting an explicit subordination of international obligations to national policies; they were unable to provide satisfactory and workable rules for state-trading; rules proposed for the 'still-born' International Trade Organization (ITO) on restrictive trade practices were not taken over into the GATT or elsewhere; and there were no conventions or arrangements to govern intra-firm trade or foreign investment.

7.5   Despite GATT's considerable success in facilitating reductions in tariff protection on manufactured products, a liberalisation associated with a period of substantial economic growth in the industrialised and subsequently the developing countries, the importance of these gaps has grown and further inadequacies in the system have emerged. Most notably, there has been diminishing compliance with the rules and principles as originally established and there have been a host of new developments, not anticipated by the original negotiators.

7.6   The 1982 Commonwealth Report on Protectionism noted that 'International trade today is evidently in large part not governed by the principles and rules formulated by the original negotiators of the GATT. A high proportion of trade takes place on a basis other than that of unconditional m.f.n. tariffs; discrimination is found both at a general level, as between members of different 'tiers' or trading blocs (OECD, EEC, etc.) and selectively, in respect of particular countries and industries. There is wholesale abuse or evasion not only of GATT principles but even of prescribed GATT rules, particularly in respect of quantitative restrictions; there is growing resort to non-tariff measures for which there are no GATT rules. Bilateralism has been substituted for the envisaged multilateral approaches to trade negotiation, policy debate and dispute settlement. As non-tariff measures have proliferated, the transparency of trade barriers has been reduced, making monitoring, surveillance and assessment of effects much more difficult. In general, much higher proportions of international trade are being 'administered' and 'managed' both by governmental and private transnational actors, than the original negotiators anticipated.'[1]

7.7   A particularly significant characteristic of these failures has been the shift away from general acceptance of the principles of multilateralism, non-discrimination and openness. The principle of multilateralism is not only threatened by the growth of bilateralism in trading arrangements but is also increasingly breached in decision-making forums and in newly established procedures such as the GATT's codes on non-tariff measures, which depart from the basic GATT principle of unconditional m.f.n. treatment.

7.8   Discrimination, which the GATT itself permitted from the outset in the case of customs unions, has grown in various ways. Apart from the growth of customs unions, notably that of the EEC, discrimination has expanded along with the use of non-tariff measures, most of which inevitably require it. A further contributor is the by now extensive range of preferential arrangements, which includes those for developing countries designed to offset their disadvantages elsewhere in the trading system. The principal form of developing country preference, the Generalised System of Preferences (GSP), was a unilateral concession by the industrialised countries, seen as an exception to the principle of non-discrimination; other preferential arrangements have also emerged, such as those for the countries associated with the EEC. The size and importance of these developing country preferences are small, however, relative to other factors affecting trade. A more substantial breach of the non-discrimination principle was the Multi-fibre Arrangement (MFA) governing textile trade and its predecessors, all of which, though negotiated in the GATT, discriminate against low-cost, usually developing country, producers.

7.9   The growing use of non-tariff protective measures, and especially 'voluntary export restraints' (VERs), has greatly reduced the openness of the system as well as increasing the role of government. The growing use of VERs since the 1960s has reflected the exercise of economic and political power not just to breach GATT provisions but to refrain from appealing to the existing international procedures as well. The smaller and weaker countries, since they had limited retaliatory capacity, found themselves with less and less voice in the management of international trade.

---

1.   *Protectionism: Threat to International Order — the impact on developing countries;* report by a Group of Experts, Commonwealth Secretariat, 1982, paragraph 2.40.

7.10 Associated with the extensive use of such measures has been increased sectoral protection that was previously limited to a few sectors such as agriculture, coal or textiles. In the 1960s and to a greater degree in the 1970s, many industries in the industrialised countries of Western Europe and North America faced increased import competition from Japan and increasingly from developing countries. In some cases, import competition, though a factor, was not the major problem of the industry.

7.11 'Industrial policies' to deal with industry-specific problems were often justified on grounds similar to those previously used for agriculture, coal or textiles. These included the regional concentration of unemployment, the security importance of maintaining the sector or the need to adjust slowly where traditional skills were involved. Pressure for such policies accelerated when unemployment generally rose to substantial proportions, and the GATT has made no provision for linking concerns about employment with those about trade and adjustment.

7.12 It can, of course, be argued that such protection may allow the industry an opportunity for reconstruction. There must be some doubt, however, whether the industry will, in fact, take advantage of the opportunity or that the measures will be temporary. Structural adjustment is usually better assisted via 'positive' measures such as grants for retraining, relocation, diversification, etc. In the present context, the important point is that, as long argued for agriculture, international discussion of measures dealing with many industrial sectors can no longer deal only with traditional trade measures and still be effective. Industrial policies as a whole now have to be considered.

7.13 More generally, efficiency requires that resources be reallocated and 'positive' adjustment take place as comparative advantage shifts. The management of international trade, whether by governments or by transnational corporations, must not be permitted to stand in the way of orderly adjustment at a reasonable pace. Wherever protection is authorised, it must be strictly time-bound and linked to adjustment measures that will ensure that it is, in fact, temporary.

7.14 In outcome, therefore, the existing international trading system differs significantly from that originally envisaged, in that adherence to collectively agreed principles and to the use of rules and pre-existing criteria to govern trading relations and dispute settlement has diminished, and direct government intervention has greatly increased.

7.15 Apart from the implications of these failures for the international financial and trading system, the trading system as originally conceived has itself been affected by a number of developments of importance over the last two decades or so.

7.16 First, as has repeatedly been stressed, a large number of newly independent countries have joined the system since the original negotiations took place. Although nominally developing countries made up the majority of the original contracting parties to the GATT, the effective influences at that time were those of the United States and a small number of other major industrialised countries. The newly independent countries did not share many of the values and objectives of the major countries which devised the system and some were not, in any case, private market economies. Again, in many developing countries, there was suspicion that liberal trading principles were likely to involve a continuation of exploitative relationships and some of this suspicion remains. Although many developing countries continue to operate substantial protective barriers, there is now greater recognition of the potential gains from an outward orientation in their development; developing countries have participated substantially in the increased openness and international interdependence of national economies, both through trade and private capital inflows. It is unfortunately partly in response to their success in export development that new protective barriers have arisen in industrialised countries.

7.17 A second new development is the growing importance of international trade in services. Recognition that this trade, now of significant global proportions, is outside the GATT's purview has led to increased effort, particularly by the United States, to bring services within the existing trading system. The question of trade in services raises many new and sensitive issues that need to be dealt with separately and openly. Part of the concern of those resisting the complete liberalisation of such trade is that many kinds of services, such as insurance, banking, transport, telecommunications and information retrieval, involve a high degree of potential intrusiveness into local culture and even sovereignty, or are at least frequently perceived to do so by industrialised as well as developing countries; in this sense such trade has characteristics distinct from that in merchandise, which is normally thought of in trade discussions. Part, however, consists of more orthodox concerns about the appropriate means of handling restrictive business practices, foreign investment, the transfer of technology and, especially, the role of transnational corporations, with all of their impacts on trade, development and international flows of income. Particularly at issue is whether these questions are best handled in the GATT or in other United Nations bodies, especially UNCTAD which has already been active in this field.

7.18 Logically, consideration of international trade in services should include labour services. Since movements of labour across national frontiers have significant effects on trade, policies toward migrants ought to be part of any international system dealing with trade and trade-related matters. As with the trade in other services, many countries perceive such issues as affecting local culture as well as sovereignty, and consequently regard conditions of international exchange of labour services as not for international negotiation.

7.19 A further development is the marked change in circumstances in the international financial system. That there were close linkages between financial and trade matters was clearly understood at Bretton Woods and Havana but the changes both in circumstances and in understanding since then have been substantial. In particular, in addition to the immediate but fundamental links between debt-servicing capacity and increased exports by debtor countries, there are structural links between interest rates, borrowing incentives and trade adjustment incentives. In the last decade the link between trade and exchange rates has assumed new importance in the context of perceived misalignments and volatility of exchange rates.

Existing Institutional Machinery

7.20 For trade the central institutional pillar for much of the post-war period has been the GATT. Despite its very creditable achievements, the GATT has gradually become less effective and credible, as is evident from declining adherence to its established principles and rules. Contributing to this declining adherence has been the growing importance of other influences on trade, such as investment policies, transnational corporations, state-trading, and restrictive business practices, and the growing complexity of linkages between trade and macro-economic and sectoral policies within national boundaries as well as outside them. Few of these matters can be dealt with effectively within the GATT, at least in its present form.

7.21 An increased role has therefore been taken by other organs, particularly by UNCTAD and the OECD, not just on matters such as restrictive business practices and trade in services, but directly on trade matters. UNCTAD is able to discuss a wide range of inter-linked issues, but has few powers of its own. It does have operative responsibility for commodity trade, as the United Nations body within which international commodity agreements (ICAs) are negotiated. The arrangements for ICAs arose originally from acceptance in the UN of that part of the Havana Charter dealing with commodities, and the GATT provides for exemptions from its rules in certain circumstances where an ICA exists. The IMF also offers finance for contributions to international buffer-stocks. Negotiations for changes in these arrangements, such as those on the Integrated Programme for Commodities (IPC) or on the Common Fund for commodities, take place largely within UNCTAD, as do trade negotiations involving developing countries, such as those on the GSP. Other bodies in the UN have other special responsibilties, such as the FAO with respect to the principles of disposal of food surpluses as aid.

7.22 The development of codes on the operations of transnational corporations has been taking place in several places, including the OECD and the UN Centre on Transnational Corporations, while at UNCTAD a code of conduct on technology transfer has been sought and a set of principles and rules governing restrictive business practices has been agreed.

7.23 The objectives of co-operation and consistency among the various institutions are normally specified when functions are initially allocated and are often prescribed in the original agreements or terms of reference. Within the constraints of the range of functions specified or seen as appropriate for each institution and of the interests of constituent groups (or of the bureaucracies themselves), a reasonable degree of collaboration has existed in many contexts. Both the GATT and the IMF articles of agreement provide for GATT/IMF co-ordination, though these arrangements are largely concerned with links between the balance-of-payments analyses of the Fund for individual countries and their trade policies. The GATT Consultative Group of Eighteen has been studying co-ordination between the GATT and IMF so far as international adjustment is concerned.

7.24 It was originally intended that UNCTAD would link the range of international economic issues: trade, services and capital flows, including development finance. It has not been able to do this as effectively as was hoped, particularly for financial issues, in part because of the role of already existing specialised agencies in these fields, and in part because of the limited acceptance of UNCTAD by the industrialised countries.

Short-term Problems

7.25 It was noted earlier that the actual or potential international financial instability that has arisen from the debt-servicing problems of many developing countries stems from various underlying factors, a major one being the deterioration in the conditions of international trade. International demand, having recovered somewhat from the global recession of the mid-1970s, fell again during 1980-82 and many products of importance to the major indebted developing countries faced collapsed prices and intensified trade barriers. Ultimately, without an expansion of exports it is not possible for debtor countries to service their debt.

7.26 Without recovery in the international economy no solution to the immediate problems of debtor countries is possible. Pursuit of appropriate domestic policies in these countries is important but no such measures are by themselves sufficient. Creditor countries have to improve the trading system and, within that, their openness to imports so that debtor countries can increase exports to service their debts.

7.27 It is crucial that there be an immediate stop to the introduction of further protectionist measures. General declarations of purpose may be necessary, and the latest ones from the Williamsburg Summit and from UNCTAD VI are welcome, but they are not enough. There must be detailed and sustained follow-up procedures. Monitoring and surveillance must be buttressed by agreed sanctions against transgressors — even if they consist of no more than authorisation for public denunciation by international secretariats.

7.28 The pressures of the moment need to be taken into account in the policies of international economic institutions, which should never be inflexibly applied despite changing circumstances. For example, although it is clearly undesirable, other things being equal, for any country to increase trade barriers, the present circumstances are exceptional. Attempts to push liberalisation too far upon financially-strapped countries — whether in the context of IMF conditionality, GATT multilateral negotiations, or in bilateral trade and financial agreements — may be misconceived in the current circumstances. Without assurances that export earnings will soon expand and barriers to external market entry will be reduced, it would be foolhardy for many countries now to undertake liberalisation programmes. For the IMF to require, as a condition of its standby arrangements, that there be liberalisation or even a standstill in trade and exchange restrictions by a borrowing country, however desirable these may be in the long-run, would seem counterproductive. Since these countries spend particularly promptly any increase in foreign exchange earnings, liberalisation would do little for international exchange but could well limit their later capacity to maintain stability and increase imports on a sustained basis. It was in recognition of these situations that the IMF articles provided for balance-of-payments restrictions.

7.29 This example illustrates the frequent difficulty of making a clear distinction between short-term and long-term policy objectives and problems. Again, it was a short-term liquidity problem that led to substantially increased borrowing from the banking system in the 1970s for primarily long-term development purposes. Possibly, too, at the same time, low real interest rates, leading to excessive borrowing from all available sources, permitted some countries to defer trade and other economic adjustments now seen as necessary. The link between financial and trading issues is therefore of major importance not only in the broader long-term sense but also in ways which emerge in apparently short-term situations.

7.30 Sustained recovery will provide the opportunity for returning to the spirit as well as the letter of the GATT. Reducing protection will simultaneously dampen inflationary pressures and stimulate productivity growth in the industrialised countries and assist in debt-servicing and development in the developing ones.

Financial/Trade Linkages

7.31 Flexible exchange rates are said to generate two general kinds of influence upon trade — one positive, the other negative. To the extent that more flexible exchange rates contribute to balance in the external accounts, the need for direct controls, in those countries employing such measures for macro-economic policy purposes, is reduced. On the other hand, the increased variability of exchange rates creates greater uncertainty for those in import-competing (and export) industries and hence may lead to increased pressures for protection; though the uncertainty effect can easily be exaggerated, given the considerable uncertainty of the previous 'fixed' exchange rate regime. The relative importance of these influences depends upon the make-up of national policy objectives (whether macro-economic or sectoral) and the policy measures typically used to achieve them.

7.32 Sustained over- or under-valuation of exchange rates can lead to protectionist pressures. An overvalued exchange rate discourages exports and encourages imports, leading to pressures for protection against imports and for export subsidies. An undervalued exchange rate may stimulate development in export and import-competing industries that, without protection, may not be sustainable once the undervaluation is removed. In both cases, protective measures are likely to persist after the exchange rates are realigned. This effect may be important if the misalignments are sustained for a significant period — and this has been argued at various times with respect to the dollar, the yen, sterling and the deutsche mark. A further problem is that the existence of exchange rate misalignments has some legitimacy as a source of complaint by affected business interests and labour unions.

7.33 Greater experience with flexible exchange rates may reduce business expectations that exchange rate misalignments are long-term phenomena, but uncertainties are likely to remain large given the difficulty of discerning, at any time, what is the appropriate real rate. Such uncertainties are likely to affect investment and development and may encourage protectionist pressures.

7.34 How these uncertainties are best resolved has been discussed above (paragraphs 3.33-3.42) but, as already indicated (paragraph 3.22), such misalignments existed even before the shift to flexible exchange rates; part of the reason for the move from fixed exchange rates was the disenchantment with the persistent imbalances in the existing parities of the dollar, the yen, sterling and the deutsche mark, and the protectionist pressures they were generating, particularly in the United States. Indeed, it has been argued that there is a close correlation between under- and over-valuation of the dollar and protectionist or liberal trade attitudes in the United States.

7.35 Whatever the methods adopted internationally with respect to the determination of exchange rates, reduction in their volatility or in the extent of misalignment will depend upon some degree of international co-ordination of national trade, exchange rate, and macro-economic policies. Trade, monetary and macro-economic policy co-ordination within nations as well as between them needs, in consequence, to be enhanced. Moves toward international co-ordination might stimulate greater domestic policy consistency.

7.36 It has been suggested earlier (paragraph 3.21-3.30) that trade, monetary and financial policies should be discussed within a common multilateral framework; and that arrangements to this end could and should be set up in the very near future. It was suggested that the IMF, World Bank, GATT and UNCTAD should jointly service a body functioning somewhat like the IMF's advisory Interim Committee, eventually evolving into the analogue of the decision-making Council authorised in the IMF's Second Amendment. In any such arrangements trade issues must not be seen as the 'second cousin' of the financial ones. And the new arrangements must not be or be seen to be an extension of the jurisdiction of the IMF into trade policy issues.

7.37 Moreover, when trade and financial issues are jointly approached there must be symmetry in the treatment of individual countries. Nothing could be more damaging to the prospect for a more integrated approach to international economic co-operation than the perception that it consists, in fact, of the addition of trade policy conditions to those already demanded of debtor countries by multilateral financial institutions, while leaving the creditor countries unaffected.

7.38 Whatever new arrangements may be agreed for integrating consideration of financial and trading questions, there will still be a need for stronger international machinery in the sphere of international production and trade.

Improving the Trading System

7.39 Despite the difficulties involved, the chances of avoiding deeper and longer economic crises in the future and of providing a trading and financial framework in which developing as well as industrialised countries can resume developmental progress, depend upon much greater international co-operation. It is critically important in the short-run for sustained economic recovery that the deterioration in the international trading environment be halted. Without such a recovery, and with the present weak international trading framework, efforts to stem protectionism are unlikely to have a chance.

7.40 It was observed earlier that the trading system was originally to be based on permanent rules and criteria for international arrangements that would reduce the likelihood of conflict and protect weaker countries from the economic and political power of the strong, as well as protecting private traders from the arbitrary intervention of governments. Although granted greater discretion than the proposed ITO or the GATT, the IMF was similarly based on a generally liberal and non-discriminatory approach. Subsequently, however, the non-discrimination principles have been substantially breached in both trade and financial affairs. Existing multilateral rules have been broken or changed informally by governments acting alone or collectively in international forums which are restricted to only some of the industrialised countries. The rules have thereby been rendered unpredictable and subject to the judgement and discretion of a few countries. Developing countries and the smaller industrialised ones have been disadvantaged in this change in the system.

7.41 The GATT in reality does little more than administer the contractual arrangements between member countries. As already noted, the gaps in the existing trade machinery are large — both as regards specific trade matters and their linkages with other trade-related questions. The changes needed to enable all important trade-related issues to be discussed together are similarly substantial. While there have been a number of amendments to the financial and trading system since the original negotiations in response to changed circumstances, there is wide acceptance that in the trade sphere these have not been sufficient.

7.42 There are now a considerable number of institutions involved in the various aspects of trade and of finance related to trade. The proliferation of institutions can be ascribed to factors ranging from the advantages of specialised bodies dealing with issues on their technical merits, rather than on politicised grounds, to the desire by developing countries for new institutions, where they can achieve a greater voice than in existing institutions usually controlled by the industrialised countries. The functionalist approach to problems tends to substitute institutions for solutions, though there are times when institutions are easier to replace than to reform. At times, too, new institutions reflect the trend to regional or other blocs and to bloc approaches to trade and trade-related questions. This has led to institutions tending to represent particular interests — the OECD representing the industrialised countries and, in the absence of a developing country equivalent, UNCTAD imperfectly serving the developing countries, with the GATT falling uneasily in between: neither group of countries fully accepts it as a multilateral body, but for opposing reasons. The present international machinery has proved inadequate to deal with the emerging trade problems. Moreover, as has been seen, existing institutional arrangements, at the national as well as the international level, unduly separate consideration of trade policy issues from consideration of international financial questions.

7.43 To some, 'trilateral' management, summitry, and small-group consensus in trade issues as in others is an appropriate direction of change. Such developments, whatever their merits, risk movement away from a multilateral, non-discriminatory and open approach; they also can involve a move away from a rule-based system to one where management by the powerful prevails.

7.44 Proposals to build upon OECD arrangements and for the selective extension of GATT principles via a so-called 'super-GATT', supposedly for like-minded liberal market economy countries, should be resisted. While such arrangements may have some short-term benefits in handling crisis situations, and may be a useful adjunct to fully multilateral bodies, they seem likely to perpetuate existing divisive arrangements of a regional or bloc nature, enhance trends to bilateralism, and downgrade the role of existing institutions and the principles of multilateralism.

7.45 In considering the need for systemic change it is necessary to consider the substantive issues and their institutional requirements. As has been seen, to halt the growth of protection is a first priority. This, as already noted, is critical to sustained recovery from recession and to stability in the international financial system; it is also necessary for continued development in the developing countries. In one sense, it can be handled within existing institutional arrangements. But to sustain it may well require more.

7.46 A major, longer-term, need is to bring all 'administered' and 'managed' trade effectively under international surveillance and internationally agreed rules and procedures. At the same time, as recognised at the Williamsburg Summit, there should be a determined effort to roll back the recent growth in protectionist non-tariff measures. Where protection is unavoidable, tariffs are a better choice. They are least damaging internationally and they are characterised by the openness and predictability needed for an effective and equitable trading system. For reasons given earlier, success in this aim is likely to require concurrent measures in the field of international monetary co-operation and probably, therefore, progress in the field of broader economic co-operation as well.

7.47 The restoration of multilateralism in decision-making, with respect to the establishment of rules, codes and procedures relating to international trade and exchange, and the settlement and management of disputes relating thereto, is basic to an effective system that is acceptable and adhered to by all. A major complaint by the developing countries, and one often voiced by the small industrialised countries as well, is their lack of effective participation in decision-making on trade or trade-related matters. It is much more difficult to persuade these countries of the system's benefits when they are not full participants in its decision-making procedures.

7.48 The principle of non-discrimination is fundamental and adherence to it must be strengthened. Although both the GATT and the IMF were based on non-discriminatory principles, major departures from those principles have been accepted or have occurred in both cases. In the GATT, not only were regional trade arrangements permitted, but major derogations have been accepted, in the MFA in particular. In international discussion of the critical need to develop a satisfactory system of 'safeguards' against market disruption, the already widespread use of discriminatory arrangements has been employed to support arguments for still more.

7.49 Certainly, although non-discrimination provisions were designed to protect the weak, the present system has done that imperfectly. Direct discrimination that now exists in trade and in exchange rate and payments mechanisms adds to indirect discrimination through lack of full developing country participation in discussions about trade, finance and reforms of the system, within and outside the IMF and the GATT. Even though never completely specified in a formal way nor adhered to in practice, the principle of non-discrimination has been an important restraint on discriminatory actions in trade and exchange likely to affect developing and other economically less powerful countries.

7.50 The question of 'graduation' is important to the reciprocity debate. While existing preferences for developing countries are probably not of great net benefit to any of them, those for the economically more advanced developing countries become less and less defensible. In due course, these countries will have to become full participants in the system, and then themselves provide preferential entry to economically less advanced developing countries. Of course, with such graduation, discrimination against them, as in the MFA or in any new 'safeguard' arrangements, would similarly be difficult to justify. Graduation should, after all, involve rights as well as obligations. The principles and procedures for graduation should be multilaterally agreed rather than be the product of a series of *ad hoc* unilateral decisions frequently influenced by short-term political objectives.

7.51 Foreign investment, although not dealt with to any significant extent within the existing international system, substantially affects the pattern of trade. Investment subsidies and the regulation of foreign investment have major trade impacts, as do the restrictive practices of investors or governments. The quesion of sovereignty is again involved and contributes to the difficulties of devising arrangements covering satisfactorily the rights and obligations of enterprises and governments with respect to their investments. Accommodation and consensus among governments need to be sought to achieve some internationally accepted and understood rules on the international trade aspects of investment, dealing amongst other things with questions of jurisdiction and extra-territoriality.

7.52 Codes on international trade in services, including labour, will also need careful consideration, since, because of their nature, the willingness to accept freer rules than at present is likely to be limited. Any such codes should not breach the general principles of non-discrimination and openness.

7.53 Although development of codes of conduct on transnational corporations and on technology transfer has been proceeding in several forums, and guidelines on restrictive business practices have been agreed, these efforts have not generally taken into account the specific impact which the codes would have on trade. Attempts should be made, therefore, to bring the codes within a GATT-type framework. As with efforts to develop appropriate measures for state-trading, the important issues with respect to any rules developed are their non-discriminatory and open operation.

7.54 Some acceptable forum for discussing industrial and agricultural policies is also needed. Its absence has been critical to the treatment of agricultural trade since the early days of the existing system. Such a forum now has potentially much wider significance, with a number of industrial products being treated in a similar way to agricultural ones.

7.55 The time has come for a major effort to strengthen and to rationalise the basic institutional structure concerning international trade, production and related activities. International institutional changes serve no purpose if there is no governmental will to change underlying policy fundamentals. It is essential to develop joint approaches and improved consultation and co-ordination among the institutions concerned with international policies in trade and trade-related fields. Already there is a joint effort between GATT and UNCTAD in export promotion through the UNCTAD/GATT International Trade Centre. This might be a model for other activities, including joint advisory and executive bodies. Such joint and co-operative activities could improve the scope for GATT and UNCTAD to be seen not as rival but as complementary institutions and facilitate a possible eventual integration of their activities in trade and trade-related fields. This could involve the emergence of an institution which incorporates not only GATT and UNCTAD but also at least some of the trade-related activities of other organisations such as the UN Centre on Transnational Corporations. Such an institution could probably serve only as an umbrella organisation with a number of semi-autonomous departments, each conceivably containing different membership and rules. Acceptance of even such a loose arrangement may take a long time before becoming politically acceptable, however logical it may be functionally. But if the international community is both to rationalise the present institutional structure in which international trade is set and to provide an effective framework with the necessary degree of comprehensiveness, ultimately an effective, policy-making ITO-type of body, with a wide-ranging mandate, would be desirable.

7.56 It must be the objective of such institutional change in the trading system to encourage the further reduction of trade barriers, the development of multilaterally agreed trading and investment rules, and adherence to the agreed arrangements. Institutional reform must also aim to prevent retrogression in the maintenance of an open trading system during periods of economic stress of the kind the international system has recently been facing. What must be sought is a more rule-oriented international trading system in which the principles of non-discrimination, multilateralism and transparency are firmly entrenched, and in which there is considerable further refinement of such codes and rules as there are to facilitate control and ultimately removal of unauthorised trade barriers. All of this must be supported and reinforced by effective dispute settlement procedures, high levels of co-ordination with the financial system and greatly enhanced macro-economic international co-operation.

Chapter 8

Contingency Plans Against Pessimistic Scenarios

Aborted Recovery and Disaster Contingency Plans

8.1 The modest economic recovery discussed at the beginning of Chapter 3 may not be sustained. The forecasts may prove wrong, as they often do. Even well co-ordinated international action in support of non-inflationary recovery may prove ineffective. On the one hand, growth may be sluggish. On the other, inflationary expectations may quickly revive and be contained only by severe monetary measures which again raise real interest rates, and hence abort the recovery.

8.2 In that event, the national and international authorities must be ready and able to implement pre-arranged contingency plans to deal with what are likely to be the two most immediate and pressing international needs: debt crises and the plight of the poorest.

The debt problem

8.3 The possible truncation of recovery in the industrialised countries, particularly if associated with higher real interest rates, holds major risks for satisfactory long-term resolution of the developing countries' debt situation. While the debt-service burden for these countries would remain high or even increase, the expansion in their exports which should result from greater economic activity could be curtailed, rendering their adjustment programmes impossible to implement. A new debt crisis would be forced on the world.

8.4 Of major concern is the large burden of relatively short-term debt accumulated by many countries in recent years as a result of the depressed state of the international economy and the adjustments imposed by oil price increases. Much of the debt is owed to private banks, in amounts and on terms and conditions which with hindsight seem commercially unjustified. This debt is a two-fold threat if recovery falters. In the first instance, its servicing would become much more difficult and virtually impossible in some cases. Even if the required debt-servicing is maintained, it would constitute a massive drain on future resources. In the second place, the existence of these large, unsecured debts poses a serious threat to depositors and shareholders in banks and other financial institutions in the major industrialised countries. In the economic conditions imagined, the possibility of default and bank failures, or fear of bank failures, would cause the sort of uncertainty which at the very least would poison the atmosphere and threaten a breakdown of confidence in the financial system.

8.5   Much of the maturing debt can, in principle, be rolled-over or rescheduled and the international financial system has already shown that it can respond quickly and responsibly to deal with cases that require international co-operation. There is, however, a legitimate view that the size of the debt problem is now so great that the risk of leaving it to be dealt with *seriatim,* crisis-by-crisis, by the international banking system is too great to run. While there is danger in allowing either lenders or borrowers to feel that their mistakes may be paid for by someone else, the seriousness of the debt problem and the fragility of the recovery require, exceptionally, some public, international reassurance that possible crises will not be allowed to escalate. This requires, as suggested in Chapter 5, the preparation of contingency plans which could be activated if the debt situation were to deteriorate further for whatever reasons, including the possible faltering of the present recovery.

8.6   The circumstances that give cause for concern encompass three conditions. First, a country or group of countries is unable, because of insufficient foreign exchange receipts on both current and capital account to repay, as normally expected, interest or principal on debt; and there is little prospect of it soon being able to do so. It may not be possible to reduce foreign exchange requirements for other uses: in other words, the country is totally illiquid and quite possibly insolvent. Secondly, the country's (or countries') creditors, notably international commercial banks, are unwilling to lend more. Thirdly, if the country, or countries, formally defaulted on or repudiated the debt, the international repercussions on both creditors and other debtors are judged to be large enough to shake the overall stability of the system. In all of this there is a large element of judgement, with the usual commercial bargaining between debtor and creditor. Nevertheless, there can be little doubt that the international financial community knows when these conditions are found and when a 'crisis' truly exists.

8.7   The contingency flows required in such an eventuality go beyond the emergency procedures of the type developed after the Mexican crisis of August 1982. Essentially, these latter procedures involve the debtor seeking short-term loans (from other governments and the BIS) to be repaid once the debtor has reached agreement with the IMF on a recovery programme. In turn the IMF assistance, for an extended period, allows the debtor to restructure its debts to commercial banks and other countries. Of course, these procedures cannot work even in the short-run if the banks reduce their net lending to the debtor; they must therefore be persuaded to continue or even to expand their lending.

8.8   Contingency plans must recognise that the commercial banks may themselves be in difficulty and therefore be unable, as distinct from being unwilling, to continue lending. (To some degree this has already occurred in the case of a number of smaller US banks.) The simplest plan is for either their own central banks or an international agency such as the IMF to buy the commercial banks' loans (at a substantial discount, to invoke a penalty) which would then be converted, with the debtor's approval, into longer-term debt at a lower rate of interest. Subsequently, the new debt, carrying the guarantee of the central bank or the IMF, could be sold on the market or taken over by another international institution. An emergency issue of SDRs might at the same time bolster confidence.

8.9   In the unlikely event that default or repudiation occurs, either before such schemes can be activated or despite their availability, the lender of last resort facilities described in Chapter 5 may have to be deployed — not to bail out insolvent commercial banks but to overcome consequent liquidity crises. In that event there must be orderly procedures for the write-off of debt; in some cases banks may have to be allowed to fail.

8.10 A difficulty with the plans for bank debt is that both debtor countries and commercial banks that are creditors of other countries not in crisis situations may try to take advantage of them. These difficulties can be reduced if the discount on the value of the loans is large enough, and if the debtor country is subjected to an approved and suitably rigorous adjustment programme. It is important to emphasise that such contingency plans are suggested purely for the management of potential disasters.

8.11 Other proposals for restructuring the short-term debt of developing countries, as was seen in Chapter 5, rely essentially on the same idea: the taking over of short-term commercial bank loans and replacing them by bonds at low rates of interest. There are several proposed variants of the basic idea. The contingency plan suggested here is designed as a stop-gap until such time as more permanent arrangements may be made.

The plight of the poorest

8.12 Assistance to the poorest countries is the second major task of a contingency plan in the event of aborted recovery. For these countries the problem is not primarily one of indebtedness: they are too poor to borrow on the market. Instead the recession has lowered the demand for their commodity exports, and reduced their commodity prices, while their import needs and prices have continued to rise. In other words, the industrialised countries' successes in reducing inflation have been achieved partly at the cost of reducing the poorest countries' terms of trade and real incomes earned from exporting. At the same time, aid in real terms has failed to increase significantly. Many of these poor countries are in a state of economic and social collapse. The political dangers are evident.

8.13 A sustained recovery, by causing a revival in the demand for commodities, and probably in their prices too, will reduce the immediate pressures on those poor countries. However, if recovery is aborted, urgent measures will be needed to deal with those already in dire straits. Contingency plans should be prepared by the major donors to allow for rapid expansion of bilateral aid on a case-by-case basis. An appropriate procedure might be for the World Bank and IMF to refer the deserving cases and their recommendations for appropriate structural adjustment policies to an *ad hoc* group of major donors who would approve allocations on a country-by-country basis. The aid would come from a special contingency fund created by the major aid donors. It could build upon the mechanism, in any case recommended above (paragraph 6.62), for emergency fast-disbursing aid to poor countries. It is obviously essential that such emergency, contingency aid should not reduce other aid flows.

A Pessimistic Longer-run Scenario

8.14 There is a respectable view that the factors that might abort the recovery are symptomatic of longer-term underlying trends which are likely to result in much slower average rates of growth in the industrialised countries, at least over the next decade or two, than have been customary over the past two or three decades. It is not possible, at least in the context of this Report, to assess the prospects for such a pessimistic scenario. But without giving any credence to such a view or assigning to it any degree of probability, it is necessary to draw attention briefly to the implications this would have on the broad thrust of our recommendations.

8.15 In such an eventuality, the traditional trickle-down view of world development, in which the prosperity of the industrialised countries helps to accelerate growth in the developing countries, would not hold and the developing countries would have to rely even more on internal sources of demand (and supply) for sustaining satisfactory and non-inflationary rates of growth. It would also call for much greater economic co-operation among developing countries on a wide front if their growth rates were to be made less dependent on what happened in the industrialised countries.

8.16 Such a pessimistic scenario would necessarily call for adjustment of internal policies in both industrialised and developing countries. It would certainly call for even greater emphasis on areas which already require much attention, e.g. continuous efforts to eliminate wasteful expenditure and to increase the efficiency of utilisation of all scarce resources, e.g. capital, managerial skills, foreign exchange, water and energy.

8.17 It has not been possible, in this already long Report, to address these questions of internal adjustment and of co-operation among developing countries in the event of a less supportive international environment. Quite clearly, however, the general principles of international co-operation to which attention has been drawn in this Report will remain valid even in the context of a more pessimistic scenario. Thus, in the context of low rates of growth, the need to roll back protection and then to maintain as free a system of trade and payments as possible would be all the greater. Considerations concerning a more efficient use of scarce resources through strengthening the forces of competition would become even more important. This is not to deny that with high rates of unemployment continuing, it would be that much more difficult politically to resist pressures for protection, unless measures are simultaneously taken to ameliorate the lot of the unemployed in the short-run and to tackle the longer-term trends that make for high rates of unemployment. But the fact remains that freedom of trade has even greater relevance when other factors that make for growth and stability are less strongly in operation. The same conclusion holds in respect of those recommendations that are addressed to greater consultation and co-ordination regarding macro-economic policies and to providing a greater degree of resilience and orderly adjustment in the face of internal and external shocks.

Chapter 9

Next Steps

9.1   This chapter suggests procedures for implementing the measures that we recommend for improvement of the international financial and trading system. Many of these recommendations require immediate attention and can be acted upon quickly within existing institutional arrangements. Others will take a little longer to accomplish, and may be thought of as relating to the near-future — say, the next two years or so. Still others relate to longer-term objectives and require considerably greater preparation. The long-term recommendations, and to some degree those for the near-future as well, require the mounting of a major process of reform.

9.2   What is required is appropriate machinery for developing a convergence of views as to what needs to be done and securing the necessary action. The situation is not helped by the compartmentalised nature of the negotiating process in the IMF and the World Bank, in the GATT and at UNCTAD, and within the wider UN framework. Recent efforts at securing a comprehensive negotiating framework have not succeeded so far. Yet there remains the need for an integrated approach to negotiations.

9.3   Any approach to such negotiations must be rooted in realism. Negotiations exclusively under a UN General Assembly umbrella are not likely either to be acceptable to the industrialised countries or, if acquiesced in under pressure, to win their enthusiastic and constructive participation. This may be regrettable, but it is a reality. Likewise, negotiations strictly under the umbrella of the Fund and the Bank are not likely to be acceptable to the developing countries as a group. In any case, the suggested negotiations necessarily link trading and financial issues and require a broader framework than the Fund and the

Bank provide. What is needed is a process which does not pre-determine issues, either expressly or by reasonable implication; which is integrated without being all-encompassing; which is credible in representation without being unwieldy; and which is action-oriented while not geared to any single institution.

9.4 Proposals for an international monetary conference — or a 'new Bretton Woods' — must be viewed against this backdrop. Earlier in this Report it was explained that the expression a 'new Bretton Woods' should be seen as no more than shorthand for a negotiating process which re-examines the world's financial and trading arrangements, as settled at Bretton Woods and Havana, in the light of their present working and of contemporary needs. We have not interpreted a 'new Bretton Woods' to imply a dismantling of the existing international economic institutions.

9.5 On that basis, the international community should now think in terms of a conference; but it is important to stress that it is a conference that will need the most careful preparation both as to substance and modalities. It should be seen as the culmination of a process rather than its initiation. Indeed, the process of preparation itself should be capable of identifying particular matters and measures on which the international community might take immediate action even in advance of the conference itself.

9.6 It is not necessary at this stage to define precisely the specific issues that the conference will address or to outline the order in which it might take them up. Although, as has been emphasised, money, finance and trade are inter-related, and an integrated approach towards them will ultimately be necessary, it may be appropriate for the conference to discuss these issues separately, beginning with money and finance, for example. These modalities will be among the matters for the preparatory phase to resolve.

9.7 The process of preparation should be undertaken on a small-group basis and must be supported by a high level of professional competence. It should, of course, draw on the work and discussions of the various international economic institutions.

9.8 There are obviously many approaches to such an international conference. We put forward a possible approach fully mindful that it is not the only one. Nor are all the individual components critical. What is critical is that there should be a systematic approach along these general lines. We believe that it provides a promising means of attaining goals, discussed in the introductory chapter to our Report, which the whole international community shares.

9.9 Our suggestion would be that informal consultations should be started to reach agreement on the following points:

1. The international community should work towards an international conference on the world's financial and trading system.

2. The preparatory process could be established through initiatives taken on an informal basis or alternatively by the Secretary-General of the United Nations on a multilaterally agreed basis.

3. The task of preparation could be entrusted in the first instance to a group of not more than, say, twenty governmental Ministers (or persons of Ministerial rank), broadly representative of the financial and trading interests of the international community, plus: the UN Director-General for International Economic Co-operation; the Managing Director of the IMF; the President of the World Bank; the Director-General of GATT; and the Secretary-General of UNCTAD.

4. The Committee might establish a Group of Deputies to carry out detailed work on their behalf and at their direction.

5. The Preparatory Group could be serviced by a small secretariat, perhaps headed by an independent professional chairman, assisted as required. Staff support could be mainly drawn from the UN, the IMF, the World Bank, the GATT and the UNCTAD, on the basis of agreement among themselves.

6. The Preparatory Group would have no executive authority. It could work strictly on the basis of consensus.

7. During the preparatory phase there should be no let-up in the continuing process of change within the individual international institutions. As consultations proceed, agreements may emerge in forms which permit early action through existing mechanisms; and such agreements should be actively encouraged.

8. The Preparatory Group should be required to make a report on the modalities and substantive issues for the conference to the UN Secretary-General not later than 12 months after it has been constituted.

Chapter 10

Summary and Recommendations

Summary

I.Introduction

10.1   When Commonwealth Finance Ministers met in August 1982, the economic scene was very dark. While there are now some signs of improvement, the goal of sustained non-inflationary growth is far from being achieved. Behind the immediate problems lie longer-term questions. Ministers accepted that while the institutional framework of the international economic system had evolved to some extent to meet changing world circumstances, the evolution had not kept pace with developments. Vast politico-economic changes had taken place and it was in this context that they saw the urgent need for a new overall examination of the trade and payments system and in particular the role of the international economic institutions.

10.2   During 1980-82 the world suffered the longest and most pervasive recession since the Second World War. The effects of the recession have been particularly severe in the non-oil exporting developing countries. Deteriorating trade performance and high interest rates have created serious debt-servicing problems for many developing countries. Required adjustment programmes in many cases pose a serious threat to their political stability and to the prospect of their resumed growth in the near future.

10.3   To judge the efficacy of the international financial and trading system, criteria are required. These exist in the form of overall objectives expressed with remarkable consistency in the articles of the

Bretton Woods institutions. They include: the encouragement of growth, the promotion of efficiency, the avoidance of price inflation, the reduction of instability and uncertainty, the promotion of appropriate adjustment, and the achievement of equity. Seen as essential to fulfilling these intentions was a system that was universal and based on certain fundamental principles: multilateralism, non-discrimination and openness. Non-discrimination does not imply uniformity of treatment, and special treatment is accorded to the poorer countries.

10.4 There have been some successes in international economic co-operation in the post-war period but there have also been failures. New problems have arisen which have pointed out systemic difficulties. Among the suggestions which have been put forward recently is a call for a 'new Bretton Woods'. This is interpreted by the Group as a call not simply for another conference but more immediately for renewed work towards agreed international objectives in a spirit of optimism and creativity. The present time is propitious for a sustained effort towards longer-term reform. Short-term problems however also require major attention.

II. Evolution of the International Economic System

10.5 The bitter experience of the 1930s and the Second World War demonstrated the need for increased international co-operation in money, finance and trade; this led to the establishment of the Bretton Woods institutions, which made important contributions to post-war reconstruction and to the sustained growth of production and trade in the 1950s and 1960s. In the monetary system a fairly stable regime of exchange rates was maintained up to the early 1970s and the capacity of the IMF to provide liquidity increased, although it remained small. At the World Bank, resources expanded and with the establishment of IDA and IFC new forms of support were introduced. The GATT pursued the principles of liberal and non-discriminatory international trade and this led to considerable progress in reducing tariff barriers to imports of manufactures. Other new institutions contributed to increased international co-operation.

10.6 Nearly forty years have passed since the establishment of the Bretton Woods institutions. Consideration of their capacity to deal adequately with the economic problems of the rest of the century and beyond requires that stock be taken of changes in the international system and responses to them.

10.7 Increased international interdependence, both a cause and a consequence of economic progress, has led to increased national vulnerability to external circumstances. Despite the evident increase in importance of the international dimensions of macro-economic problems, solutions continued to be pursued almost wholly through independent national policies. Governments took on greater roles in national economies than had originally been anticipated; domestic policies relating to resource allocation and other matters carried implications beyond national borders.

10.8 There are now far more independent countries than at the time of Bretton Woods and the world has acquired a multipolar character. Developing countries, only marginally involved in the creation and early evolution of the Bretton Woods institutions, are now of substantial economic importance. In the 1970s joint action by the oil-exporting countries enlarged their role in the international economic system; some of them emerged as capital surplus countries. These various developments have added to the complexity of international decision-making.

10.9 The centrally planned economies are becoming increasingly linked with the market economies in trade and capital flows. There is renewed interest in their participation in the IMF and the GATT. As non-market economies, however, they pose special problems.

10.10 The emergence and persistence of inflationary expectations have created doubts about regaining full employment, at least in the short-term. Without controlling inflation, an effective, equitable and sustainable international economic system is likely to be more difficult to achieve.

10.11 Oil price shocks and severe recessions have added new dimensions to balance of payments problems, for which longer periods of adjustment are required. The multilateral financial institutions provided increased finance, but this was far from adequate. The new requirements were met largely by the commercial banks. This unplanned growth in bank finance, together with the continuing inadequacy of the international institutions in facilitating structural adjustment, had far-reaching consequences for the international financial system.

10.12 With the emergence of floating currencies, the degree of variability of nominal exchange rates greatly exceeded expectations. Volatile short-term capital flows have led to persistent overshooting and apparent misalignment. Exchange rate instability and periods of weakness of the dollar have led to a reserve asset diversification. A multi-currency reserve system has emerged. Frequent shifts into and out of reserve currencies have complicated the management of domestic monetary policy and aggravated exchange rate instability.

10.13 There is increasing concern over issues not adequately provided for in the GATT, such as trade in agricultural products, international commodity price instability, state-trading, intra-corporate trade, restrictive business practices, and non-tariff barriers to trade. Unforeseen changes in international trade include the expansion of governmental involvement in domestic sectoral policies and the growth of preferential trading blocs. Non-tariff barriers to trade and other forms of protection have been encouraged by reduced growth and severe recession, creating major uncertainties for traders and investors and for the servicing of external debt. Further uncertainty in the international economy has been created by developments in the energy sector, where confidence has declined in the ability of the oil market to offer stable prices and security of supply.

10.14 The effects of the recession have encouraged already existing tendencies towards greater resort to nationalistic and defensive policies. As countries have struggled with their own problems, there has been a relative neglect of those of the world economy and a decline in support for internationalism and multilateralism. The provision of adequate international liquidity and the attainment of aid targets have particularly suffered in consequence.

III. Recovery and Improved Stabilisation Policies for the Future

10.15 The second oil price rise necessitated a particularly difficult and painful process of economic adjustment. The recession was undoubtedly deepened by the adoption of deflationary monetary and fiscal policies by the major industrialised countries in an effort to absorb the oil price rise and reduce the actual and expected inflation. It has had many disturbing consequences. Althogh recovery will not solve all the problems that have emerged, it will be a substantial step towards removing the threat of a major international financial crisis. However, sustainable non-inflationary recovery will be difficult to achieve and will require improvements in the international financial and trading system.

10.16 Effective co-ordination of national economic policies of the major industrialised countries is necessary to sustain and enhance the recovery. It is to be hoped that the 1983 Williamsburg Declaration on Economic Recovery will be effectively translated into policy. Consultations must ensure that macro-economic policies in the major countries are mutually consistent; a sustained recovery seems unlikely to materialise if real rates of interest rise or even remain at their current levels. Co-ordinated international action must address the avoidance of renewed inflation, crises in international debt and liquidity, and increasing protection and competitive devaluation.

10.17 Prime objectives in reforming the international system must be improved stabilisation mechanisms and contra-cyclical policies, together with improved protection for those most affected when instabilities and shocks nevertheless persist. Policies to secure stabilisation include both automatic and discretionary components. The provision of adequate liquidity and improved regimes for the flow of capital and trade can act as automatic stabilising factors at the international level.

10.18 Discretionary contra-cyclical policies are inherently more difficult to agree upon, not only internationally but also nationally. There is now less confidence in ability to 'fine tune' macro-economic decision-making. While realism requires that primary emphasis be placed upon national economic-policy decisions, countries can attempt through consultations to increase mutual consistency in their policies and to reduce arbitrariness and unilateralism in decision-making. The impact on the rest of the world has to be kept in mind in the formulation of monetary policies in the major industrialised countries.

10.19 Even when there is broad agreement over the general direction of macro-economic policy, independently formulated national expansionary or deflationary policies when aggregated are unlikely to achieve agreed objectives. Consultation and co-ordination at least among the major countries are necessary if the desired objectives are to have a good chance of being attained. When national policy-makers in major countries disagree as to the desirable direction of overall macro-economic policy, consultation is still useful for narrowing differences and minimising potentially harmful consequences.

10.20 A principal concern in international macro-economic policy consultation and co-ordination is that of promoting smooth and equitable adjustment to imbalances in international payments. Exchange rates are fundamental to the external adjustment process. With internationally mobile capital and increasing economic interdependence, exchange rate questions cannot be separated from monetary, fiscal and trade policy issues. Co-ordinated macro-economic policies will not function effectively unless the whole range of national macro-economic objectives and policy instruments are viewed together. Greater emphasis needs to be given to consultations on the links between trade policies and fiscal/monetary/exchange rate actions. The meeting of trade ministers with finance ministers before the Williamsburg Summit is a welcome precedent upon which further consultations, preferably of a more multilateral character, should be built.

10.21 There has been some improvement in the process of consultation. Since the 1982 Versailles Summit, the Managing Director of the IMF has participated in G5 discussions of economic policies. At Williamsburg, the participants declared their intention to increase multilateral co-operation with the Fund in its surveillance activities. Since the effects of the economic policies of G5 countries extend well beyond these countries' own borders and legitimacy requires wider participation, these policies should be discussed in a more widely representative forum. A forum jointly served by the IMF, the World Bank, GATT and UNCTAD seems appropriate to consider trade and finance issues together. Modest amendments to the present operating procedures of the Interim Committee of the IMF — expanding its participation and its agenda, and increasing the frequency of its meetings — might permit an immediate start in this direction.

10.22 Co-operation among the monetary authorities of the major industrialised countries is essential to the task of smoothing perverse short-term exchange rate volatility and reducing 'disorderly conditions' in foreign exchange markets. This typically involves monetary authorities in 'leaning against the wind'.

10.23 To achieve appropriate foreign exchange rates over the medium-term, policy-makers should work in terms of real effective exchange rate 'target zones' or guidelines rather than more precise exchange rate targets. There is a clear role for the IMF in assessing and advocating such guidelines or target zones for its major members, and keeping under review, in particular, the five SDR 'basket' currencies. An increased and active role for the IMF in exchange rate surveillance could promote the long-standing objective of increased symmetry of balance-of-payments adjustment. An exchange rate regime highlighting guidelines or target zones for real exchange rates of the major currencies supported by improved macro-economic policy co-ordination could constitute a significant improvement over the present disordered and anchorless exchange rate regime. It is probably futile to seek to develop an improved exchange rate regime, however, in the absence of improved macro-economic policy co-ordination.

10.24 Renewed efforts to stabilise the prices of primary products should be an important element of comprehensive contra-cyclical policies at the international level. The recent decline in commodity prices — reaching their lowest levels in half a century — has affected the import and debt-service capacity of the primary producing countries, thus deepening the recession. Policies to reduce macro-economic instability and trade barriers in industrialised countries will help in the reduction of commodity price fluctuation.

10.25   Lack of finance is hindering progress in negotiating international commodity agreements. The implementation of UNCTAD's Common Fund for commodities would be useful but not adequate. The IMF should now consider financing nationally-held stocks of commodities. New price stabilising mechanisms which are less difficult to negotiate and administer should be explored. There is a need also to establish an effective price stabilising International Grains Arrangement and better co-ordination in international arrangements concerned with stabilising food prices and providing food aid.

10.26   Oil is by far the most important item in world commodity trade. Sharp increases in its price have created two major shocks to the global economy in the last ten years. The present time may be propitious for efforts to secure an oil price stabilisation arrangement. This could be an important part of an improved international financial and trading system. Failing establishment of such an arrangement, multilateral stock management and supply security arrangements will have to be developed.

10.27   The countries most vulnerable to global economic shocks should be provided with protection. Ideally, these countries should be able to draw on a facility from which they would obtain compensating external financial resources when events beyond their control cause a reduction in their import capacity. For the poorest countries shortfalls in import capacity should be made-up by grants.

IV. International Liquidity and the IMF

10.28   Machinery to ensure an adequate and appropriately distributed supply of international liquidity is a fundamental requirement of an effectively functioning international monetary system. While adjustment is essential in cases of fundamental disequilibrium, inadequate liquidity can breed a cumulative process of competitive devaluation, protectionism and beggar-my-neighbour policies as countries struggle to restore national balance in difficult global conditions. In present circumstances inadequate liquidity could abort global recovery and even bring on a depression; yet too much liquidity could reignite inflation.

10.29   Sharp declines in global (non-gold) reserves in recent years, together with the drying up of commercial bank financing, have made the increase and control of liquidity a matter of urgency. The maldistribution of reserves between countries, particularly the inadequacy of liquidity available to poorer countries, has reinforced the case for review.

10.30 In the post-war years, liquidity creation, its composition and its distribution have been largely determined by the balance-of-payments position of the United States and, since 1971, by commercial bank credits. The IMF's role in the provision and control of liquidity has been marginal, although its influence is greater than indicated by its direct contribution to financing alone. The most obvious means to achieve increased stability and predictability in the provision of international liquidity is through the IMF.

10.31 The IMF has nevertheless taken some important initiatives in recent years, including the recent agreement to increase quotas by 47.5 per cent and provide wider access to enlarged GAB resources. Implementation now requires prompt legislative action. GAB resources should be available to all members on equal terms as a normal supplement to IMF resources, and rules governing these matters should be clarified. It is likely that, pending the implementation of these increases, the IMF will be short of resources. Even though the preferred route for increasing its resources remains quota increases, all possibilities of borrowing by the Fund must be kept open to meet this gap as well as any future needs that might arise. Fund resources may still be inadequate after implementation of increases in quota and GAB resources. Despite the increase in quotas, there is no justification for reducing maximum access limits.

10.32 The procedures for IMF quota reviews themselves need improvement. Quotas could, for instance, be reviewed every three years or allowed to grow at some pre-agreed rate related to the growth of world trade and payments for up to, say, ten years at a time, with additional selective increases negotiated at shorter intervals. Future arrangements will also need to consider the relative distribution of quotas.

10.33 IMF credit is provided unconditionally or with low-conditionality up to certain specified limits, beyond which it is conditional on meeting certain pre-conditions and subsequently attaining performance targets. The poorest countries require more low-conditionality IMF credit than they have been getting. The Compensatory Financing Facility (CFF) could be an important means of increasing such credit.

10.34 With only modest amendments, the CFF could meet more adequately the liquidity needs of poorer countries. Even after taking the enlarged quotas into account, there is an urgent need to raise substantially the limits of CFF drawings. These should be related to shortfalls rather than to quotas. Other improvements involve taking account of import price changes; calculating shortfalls appropriately in periods of prolonged recession; and increasing flexibility in the repayment period. Insofar as the CFF is designed to compensate for temporary shortfalls, conditionality has no relevance. Because the CFF works contra-cyclically, SDR allocations seem an obvious and non-inflationary means of financing its expansion. As a logical extension, the IMF could provide low-conditionality credit in cases of non-reversible shocks, with finance offered on a tapering basis over, say, a four-year period.

10.35 Annual allocations of SDRs should resume forthwith in order to supplement the present level of liquidity, improve the composition of reserves and promote a more orderly and predictable system of liquidity creation. If from time to time there is an excess of liquidity, SDR allocations can continue via the establishment of a Substitution Account.

10.36 The objective of an SDR-based reserve system remains desirable for the longer-term. Some measures have been taken and still others are possible in its furtherance. The use of SDRs as a unit of account outside the Fund could be promoted by such means as allowing private holdings of SDRs, creating SDR clearing arrangements, and fostering an inter-bank market in SDRs. A merger of the IMF's General Account with its SDR Account would greatly simplify IMF lending and have important consequences for the future role of the IMF.

10.37 Future disputes could be minimised and early resort to the Fund encouraged by a sensitive country-specific application of conditionality. There should be primary reliance on balance-of-payments targets rather than on monetary ones, and external prescriptions as to the precise character of domestic credit and fiscal management should be minimised. Formal performance targets, if retained, should be made more flexible through agreed margins of deviation, linked in a pre-agreed fashion to key exogenous variables, or be waived more readily as appropriate. Inadequate performance should trigger a review mission whose brief would be to form an overall view of progress and would not necessarily lead to curtailment of lending.

10.38 In general, conditionality should be shaped more by the professional judgement of the staff of the Fund and the World Bank than by the political influence of the Executive Boards; while weighted voting may be of relevance to such basic issues as size of quotas or SDR allocations, it is less so for determining appropriate policies for a country at any particular time. Greater use could also be made of outside experts.

10.39 Improved Fund/Bank arrangements are called for in Extended Fund Facility/Structural Adjustment Loan operations; while the design of adjustment policies should evolve through a joint process involving staff from the Fund and the Bank, a desirable formal step would be for both institutions to assume, and declare, a joint responsibility for the relevant adjustment programmes. In the long-run, a new lending entity could evolve by merging the EFF and SAL facilities.

V. Commercial Lending and Debt Management

10.40 Since the 1970s commercial banks have assumed a large role in international capital flows. Between 1973 and mid-1982 45 per cent of non-OPEC developing countries' deficits were financed by net banking inflows. But reliance on this form of external finance has brought problems for borrowers. Easy access to such credit encouraged some countries to postpone adjustment. Later, the recession, high interest rates and short maturities increased debt-servicing problems. Borrowing countries became increasingly vulnerable to fluctuations in market confidence and there has been a withdrawal by banks in the face of debt crises. These problems have led to a spate of reschedulings. In the ten months to June 1983 the value of cross-border debt being re-negotiated was over twenty times larger than in any previous year. As many as forty countries with outstanding debt of around $250 billion in mid-1982 are reported to be involved in rescheduling or are in substantial payments arrears.

10.41 Bank lending to non-oil developing countries halved in 1982 with the decline being very steep in the latter half of the year. Maturities have shortened. About a half of outstanding bank loans to developing countries now have a maturity of less than one year. In the meantime deficits continue to remain at high levels.

10.42 Confidence needs to be restored in the creditworthiness of the major debtor developing countries. Current account deficits must be reduced and reserves rebuilt. Resolution of the current problems depends substantially on global recovery. In the meantime, banks must be persuaded to maintain and sometimes to increase their exposure in developing countries. The various large-scale debt restructuring schemes suggested to help banks and developing countries escape from debt-created illiquidity do not seem to be practical at this juncture. They should be developed as contingency plans to be used if the situation deteriorates dramatically.

10.43 Over the past eighteen months co-ordinated action on the part of the major central banks, the BIS and the IMF has been effective in handling the debt crises. Even with improvements in liquidity, there may nevertheless, and possibly quite soon, be further problems. Longer-term and regularised procedures must be devised to reduce the fears and uncertainties that have characterised recent debt crises.

10.44 Policy improvements could be made in several areas. The debt rescheduling procedures evolved recently, in which the IMF played a critical role, need to be made less *ad hoc*; uniformity of approaches between different categories of creditors and of treatment between different debtor countries would help. A larger role for the World Bank could contribute to a longer-term perspective. Paris Club arrangements could be extended beyond the customary twelve to twenty-four months.

10.45 It should eventually be possible to develop general principles and guidelines for the rescheduling of private and official debt. Improved information on evolving credit positions could reveal funding difficulties in advance of severe crises. It is also necessary to achieve concerted action by creditor banks, including the smaller banks whose exposure may be limited. It would be helpful if central banks harmonised regulations concerning the provision for bad and doubtful debts. There is at present effectively no lender of last resort (lolr) facility. Supervisory and lolr responsibilities are linked. The Basle Concordat covers supervisory responsibilities and not specifically lolr responsibilities. The establishment by the private banks of a 'safety net' of their own faces difficulties. The establishment of a fully fledged international lolr, however desirable in principle, is some way off; agreements defining supervisory responsibilities more carefully, along with arrangements on lines of assistance between central banks, in which the US Federal Reserve must necessarily play a crucial role, are therefore necessary.

10.46 Better information will improve the process of credit risk appraisal and early warning. Reliable and consolidated debt data are still inadequately reported. The debt reporting systems of the BIS and the World Bank need to be expanded and speeded up. The establishment by the commercial banks of the Institute of International Finance (IIF) could improve information exchange among them. While the danger of breaching confidentiality limits the extent to which the IMF and the World Bank can co-operate with the commercial banks in this area, the establishment of the IIF could make co-operation easier.

VI. Long-term Finance for Development

10.47 Market mechanisms do not automatically provide adequate long-term capital flows nor do they result in an adequate balance in its distribution. The restoration of confidence in the financial system is crucial to increasing the volume of private long-term flows. Even then, systemic problems will remain. There is an immediate need to maintain credit flows to countries in debt difficulties and to increase concessional flows to poorer nations. In the longer-term it will be desirable to establish a more appropriate and stable pattern of international capital flows for development. A smaller relative role for commercial bank finance is desirable and this requires an increase in other flows.

10.48 For middle-income countries, a number of proposals have been made to improve access to bond markets. These schemes deserve further technical exploration and, where appropriate, official support. However, bond issues by developing countries are unlikely to expand significantly in the 1980s.

10.49 Foreign private direct investment can play a more significant role. Initiatives should be taken to improve the investment climate and negotiations completed for the establishment of effective codes of conduct. Investment insurance arrangements should be expanded and improved; appropriate bilateral investment treaties and agreed mechanisms for the settlement of investment disputes should be encouraged. The desired new pattern of flows requires increased emphasis on longer maturities but also on risk-sharing through equity-type forms of finance. The World Bank Group and in particular the IFC can be an important initiator of ideas in this area.

10.50 Export credits are an additional source of funds, with benefits for developing countries but also some drawbacks. Facilities in developing countries should be encouraged and assisted to tap external sources of finance.

10.51 The multilateral development banks (MDBs), including their soft-loan funds, have an important role and position in the international financial system; they are an extremely valuable source of long-term finance for development. Private and official sources of such finance should not be seen as alternatives; expanding the MDBs is likely to encourage increased private capital flows. The MDBs help to overcome imperfections in capital markets. They currently face serious problems in securing the additional resources necessary to effect an increased lending programme.

10.52 Under its existing lending programme, the World Bank's planned commitments show no real increase. Bank management is proposing an annual increase in commitments to 5 per cent in real terms by the mid-1980s. A selective capital increase of around $20 billion would permit such a programme. Even though actual subscriptions would not be required until later in the decade, it is important that early agreement be reached to this increase. World Bank capital would need to be expanded again after the mid-1980s to enable the Bank to increase its lending capacity.

10.53 IDA is facing a serious crisis in securing resources and a real threat to its whole future. It is vital that commitments to complete the $12 billion IDA VI be honoured in full by June 1984; that negotiations relating to the Seventh Replenishment be expedited so that it can commence on time; and that the level of contributions should be such as to secure real increases in resources flowing to the low-income countries.

10.54 The new co-financing initiatives announced by the World Bank to assist in maintaining commercial flows are to be welcomed, provided they do not prejudice normal World Bank lending. Co-financing must assist in securing additional lending. This could be helped by the encouragement it gives for the involvement of smaller commercial banks in lending to developing countries.

10.55 The IFC could play an expanded role in securing more private long-term and equity capital for development. Consideration should be given to an early expansion in IFC's capital.

10.56 The regional and sub-regional development banks are subject to similar financial constraints as the World Bank. The relative roles of the regional banks and the World Bank and the appropriate division of functions between them should be examined. The World Bank should consider expanding its support for regional and sub-regional banks. There are a number of areas to which these banks could give special attention.

10.57 Official Development Assistance (ODA) is a crucial source of finance for the low-income developing countries and for small states. Events of recent years have heightened the urgent need for increased ODA; in present circumstances the adjustment efforts of many countries, unless supported by concessional and quick-disbursing funds, will not succeed. The level of ODA from the industrialised countries is collectively only a little over half the agreed target of 0.7 per cent of GNP. Aid from the OPEC countries, while proportionately much higher, has been declining. Aid flows are being squeezed by donors' budgetary constraints and their distribution is being further distorted by increased attention to strategic and commercial considerations in allocating aid.

10.58 Aid targets should be refined and ways explored of realising the 0.7 per cent target before the end of the 1980s. Account could be taken of donors' varying capacities to contribute. It is vital that the targets agreed at the 1981 UN Conference on the Least Developed Countries be fulfilled.

10.59 Multilateral aid is provided more efficiently and directed more effectively at areas of internationally agreed need than is bilateral aid. Its relative decline should be reversed. The decline is adversely affecting IFAD and the UNDP as well as the multilateral development banks. A renewed commitment to multilateral approaches to financial and technical co-operation is called for.

10.60 The impact of existing aid flows could be improved by untying and by the provision of more programme aid. The poorest and smallest states would benefit particularly from immediate increases in quick-disbursing finance. Simplification and standardisation of aid procedures and improved consultations between donors would also help, as would improved arrangements for the multilateral discussion of aid issues on a regular basis. As for the longer-term, aid ought to be put on a more predictable and assured basis.

VII. An Effective and Integrated Regime for International Trade

10.61 Malfunction in the international trading system and inadequate co-ordination between trade and financial policies have contributed significantly to global economic difficulties.

10.62 There has been diminishing compliance with the rules and principles of the GATT; a proliferation of non-tariff measures; and a growing trend towards 'managed' trade and away from the original principles of multilateralism, non-discrimination and transparency. The gaps in the original system, for example in the areas of agricultural trade, state-trading, intra-firm trade and restrictive practices, have grown more important. There have also been a number of developments not foreseen at the outset, including the increasing importance of services, the growth of industrial policies, and the developments in international finance which have made links between trade and finance more complex and of greater significance.

10.63 Although GATT has remained the central institutional pillar of the trading system and has achieved considerable success in facilitating reductions in tariff protection, it has gradually become less effective. An increasing role has been taken by other agencies including UNCTAD and the OECD, not only in trade matters but also in trade-related questions.

10.64 Trade in services is of growing importance. International policies to deal with issues in this area, including those concerned with labour services, raise many new and sensitive matters that need to be dealt with separately and openly. They involve a high degree of potential intrusiveness into local cultures and sovereignty.

10.65 In the short-term the deterioration in the conditions of international trade has been a major cause of the debt-servicing problems experienced by many developing countries. Without recovery in the international economy no solution to the immediate problems of these countries is possible. It is of crucial importance that there be an immediate halt to the increase in protection. General declarations are insufficient. There must be detailed and sustained follow-up procedures. Attempts to push liberalisation upon financially-strapped countries, whether in the context of IMF conditionality, GATT multilateral negotiations or bilateral arrangements, may be misconceived in current circumstances. Without assurance that export earnings will expand, it would be foolhardy for many countries to undertake liberalisation programmes now.

10.66 Sustained recovery will provide the opportunity for a return to the spirit as well as to the letter of the GATT. There should be a determined effort to roll back protection. Reducing protection will dampen inflationary pressures, stimulate productivity and assist debt-servicing.

10.67 To the extent that they contribute to balance in the external accounts, flexible exchange rates diminish the need for direct controls. But increased volatility of exchange rates creates uncertainty in trade and hence may lead to increased pressures for protection. Sustained over- or under-valuation of exchange rates can have the same effect. Reduction in the volatility of exchange rates, however, will depend upon some degree of international co-ordination of national trade, exchange rate and macro-economic policies. Such co-ordination also needs to be enhanced at the national level.

10.68 The suggestions for international co-ordination, put forward in Chapter 3, should not lead to reducing trade issues to a subordinate status. An integrated approach to trading and financial issues emphasises the need for symmetry in the treatment of individual countries, debtor or creditor.

10.69 GATT in reality does little more than administer contractual arrangements between member countries. The gaps in the existing trade machinery are large, in spite of the proliferation of institutions involved in some aspect of trade or of finance related to trade. Policy co-ordination and the adoption of measures among small groups of major countries, whatever their merits, are not a solution in themselves. They risk moving away from the multilateral, non-discriminatory approach. Proposals for a 'super-GATT' should likewise be resisted on these grounds. Rather, the time has come for a major effort to strengthen and to rationalise the basic multilateral institutional structure in the field of trade, production and related activities. Existing arrangements for co-operation between GATT and UNCTAD suggest how joint approaches and improved consultation and co-ordination can be developed. An umbrella institution incorporating them both, together with at least some of the other trade-related activities within the UN system, might eventually emerge. An effective multilateral policy-making body with a wide-ranging mandate would provide the required comprehensive framework to deal with the problems of the trade regime.

VIII. Contingency Plans Against Pessimistic Scenarios

10.70 International and national agencies must be ready to take prompt action to deal with the two most likely immediate international needs, should recovery not be sustained: debt crises and the plight of the poorest. Contingency plans should be prepared in advance.

10.71 The faltering of recovery, especially if associated with higher real interest rates, carries major risks in the field of debt. Debt-servicing for many countries would then be virtually impossible or would impose grave strains. Default or bank failures, threatened or realised, could cause a breakdown of confidence in the international financial system.

10.72 There is a legitimate view that the debt problem is now so serious and recovery so fragile that the problem cannot safely be left in the hands of the international banking system. A situation can develop where the type of emergency procedure developed after the Mexican crisis of August 1982 cannot be adopted, since the banks may be unable to continue lending. The simplest contingency plan would be for central banks or an international agency to buy the banks' loans, at a discount, and convert them, with the debtors' approval, into longer-term debt at a lower rate of interest. Subsequently the new debt, carrying the guarantee of the central bank or the international agency, could be sold on the market. Should default occur before or despite such schemes, lender of last resort facilities may have to be employed. Such contingency plans are suggested purely for the management of potential disasters and are only a stop-gap until more permanent arrangements are made.

10.73 Many of the poorest countries are already in dire straits. In the absence of sustained recovery urgent measures will be needed to assist them. Contingency plans by the major donors should allow for rapid expansion of bilateral aid on a case-by-case basis. Such cases might be referred to an *ad hoc* group of major donors by the World Bank or the IMF, along with recommendations for appropriate structural adjustment policies.

10.74 An alternative pessimistic scenario is where the recovery is aborted by factors symptomatic of longer-term underlying trends which result in continued slow growth in the industrialised countries. In such an economic environment, developing countries could rely less on trickle-down effects and would have to depend more on internal sources of demand (and supply) and on greater economic co-operation among themselves. Internal adjustment in both industrialised and developing countries would also be required. The general principles of international co-operation would, however, remain valid. The need to roll back protection and maintain as free a system of international trade and payments as possible, for example, would be all the greater, although political pressures for protection would be stronger.

IX. Next Steps

10.75 Many of the recommendations made in this Report can be acted on quickly within existing institutional arrangements. Others will take longer to accomplish. Those in the longer-term will require the mounting of a major process of reform.

10.76 Securing agreement on what needs to be done is hampered by the compartmentalised nature of the negotiating process. An integrated but realistic approach is required, specifically a process neither exclusively under the auspices of the UN General Assembly nor strictly under those of the Fund and the Bank. The process moreover must necessarily link trading and monetary and financial issues.

10.77 The international community should now think in terms of a conference, but this should be seen as the culmination of a process rather than its initiation. It would require the most careful preparation. This process might, in the first instance, be entrusted to a preparatory group of not more than twenty broadly representative persons of ministerial rank plus the heads of the relevant international agencies. As consultation proceeds in the preparatory group, agreements may emerge in forms which permit early action through existing institutions. Not more than twelve months after it has been constituted, the group should report to the UN Secretary-General on the modalities and the substantive issues for the conference.

Major Recommendations

10.78 Many of the major recommendations of the Report have been included in the above summary, but together with others their main thrust is briefly set out below in terms of a possible time-frame for implementation.

(i)   *Immediate*

With a view to
— supporting economic recovery;
— providing sufficient liquidity from official and private sources to developing countries;
— alleviating the plight of the poorer countries; and
— preparing for discussion of international economic reform:

Increase co-ordination of macro-economic policies (3.5, 3.7, 3.25, 7.35)

Halt protection (7.27, 7.39, 7.45)

Maintain flow of private and official credit to countries in debt difficulties (5.8, 5.20, 6.3, 8.7, 8.8)

Complete current IMF quota increase with unchanged access limits (4.18, 4.24)

Complete GAB enlargement with broadened access (4.19)

Resume issue of SDRs (4.35)

Complete IDA VI contributions and agree on IDA VII at an increased real level (6.35, 6.39)

Authorise increased World Bank lending (6.23, 6.28, 6.31)

Begin emergency programme assistance to poorer countries (6.52, 6.62, 8.13)

Draw up contingency arrangements against the possibility of an aborted world recovery (8.2)

Start preparatory discussion for an international conference on the financial and trading system (9.4 to 9.9)

With a view to
— promoting sustained non-inflationary growth;
— stabilising the international economy;
— promoting greater efficiency in resource use through trade and exchange;
— ensuring the adequacy of international resource flows for development; and
— increasing the efficiency of international economic institutions, both individually and collectively:

Improve exchange rate stability under IMF surveillance (3.33, 3.36, 3.41)

Regularise SDR issues, with substitution if necessary (4.35, 4.36)

Improve system for review of IMF quotas (4.21 to 4.23)

Improve the IMF compensatory financing facility (4.30 to 4.34)

Reform IMF conditionality (4.44 to 4.47, 4.53, 4.54)

Dismantle trade barriers, restore adherence to GATT undertakings and improve the functioning of GATT (7.13, 7.46 to 7.48)

Renew attempts to seek oil price stabilisation and security of supply (3.57, 3.58)

Encourage direct investment and other medium- and long-term capital flows to developing countries to reduce the relative role of commercial bank financing (6.4, 6.5, 6.9 to 6.19, 6.23, 6.26, 6.28, 6.43)

Increase lending capacity of World Bank (6.31, 6.32)

Move towards agreed aid targets, including an increase in the proportion for the poorer countries (6.53 to 6.57)

Protect the poorest countries' import capacity (3.62, 4.30, 4.31)

Establish a multilateral forum to discuss trade, money, finance and macro-economic policies (3.26 to 3.30, 7.36)

Pursue substantive discussion of long-run improvements to the international financial and trading system (9.1 to 9.9)

(iii) *Long-term*

With a view to reforming the system so as to provide a more durable basis for achieving fundamental aims of economic policy — non-inflationary growth, efficiency, stability and equity in the international system:

Reduce cyclical instability and the risk of shocks in the system (3.13, 4.47 to 4.54, 5.15, 5.24, 6.60)

Improve multilateral control of international liquidity and develop the SDR as the principal reserve asset (4.14, 4.37)

Increase symmetry in balance-of-payments adjustment as between surplus and deficit countries, and between reserve centres and other countries; and strengthen the IMF's role in adjustment processes (3.40, 7.37)

Stabilise commodity prices (3.43, 3.51 to 3.53)

Establish regular provision of official development assistance (6.39, 6.64, 6.65)

Develop a stronger framework for world trade, production and related activities (7.36 to 7.38, 7.51 to 7.56)

Appendix I

Purposes of Major International Economic Institutions

A. International Monetary Fund

Article 1

The purposes of the International Monetary Fund are:

'a) To promote international monetary co-operation through a permanent institution which provides the machinery for consultation and collaboration on international monetary problems.

b) To facilitate the expansion and balanced growth of international trade, and to contribute thereby to the promotion and maintenance of high levels of employment and real income and to the development of the productive resources of all members as primary objectives of economic policy.

c) To promote exchange stability, to maintain orderly exchange arrangements among members, and to avoid competitive exchange depreciation.

d) To assist in the establishment of a multilateral system of payments in respect of current transactions between members and in the elimination of foreign exchange restrictions which hamper the growth of world trade.

e) To give confidence to members by making the general resources of the Fund temporarily available to them under adequate safeguards, thus providing them with opportunity to correct maladjustments in their balance of payments without resorting to measures destructive of national or international prosperity.

f) In accordance with the above, to shorten the duration and lessen the degree of disequilibrium in the international balances of payments of members.'

B. World Bank Group

1. International Bank for Reconstruction and Development

Article 1

The purposes of the Bank are:

'a) To assist in the reconstruction and development of territories of members by facilitating the investment of capital for productive purposes, including the restoration of economies destroyed or disrupted by war, the reconversion of productive facilities to peacetime needs and the encouragement of the development of productive facilities and resources in less developed countries.

b) To promote private foreign investment by means of guarantees or participations in loans and other investments made by private investors; and when private capital is not available on reasonable terms, to supplement private investment by providing, on suitable conditions, finance for productive purposes out of its own capital, funds raised by it and its other resources.

c) To promote the long-range balanced growth of international trade and the maintenance of equilibrium in balances of payments by encouraging international investment for the development of the productive resources of members, thereby assisting in raising productivity, the standard of living and conditions of labour in their territories.

d) To arrange the loans made or guaranteed by it in relation to international loans through other channels so that the more useful and urgent projects, large and small alike, will be dealt with first.

e) To conduct its operations with due regard to the effect of international investment on business conditions in the territories of members and, in the immediate postwar years, to assist in bringing about a smooth transition from a wartime to a peace-time economy.'

2. International Finance Corporation

Article I

'The purpose of the Corporation is to further economic development by encouraging the growth of productive private enterprise in member countries, particularly in the less developed areas, thus supplementing the activities of the International Bank for Reconstruction and Development (hereinafter called 'the Bank'). In carrying out this purpose, the Corporation shall:

(i) in association with private investors, assist in financing the establishment, improvement and expansion of productive private enterprises which would contribute to the development of its member countries by making investments, without guarantee of repayment by the member government concerned, in cases where sufficient private capital is not available on reasonable terms;

(ii) seek to bring together investment opportunities, domestic and foreign private capital, and experienced management; and

(iii) seek to stimulate, and to help create conditions conducive to, the flow of private capital, domestic and foreign, into productive investment in member countries.'

3. International Development Association

Preamble

' ... That mutual co-operation for constructive economic purposes, healthy development of the world economy and balanced growth of international trade foster international relationships conducive to the maintenance of peace and world prosperity;

That an acceleration of economic development which will promote higher standards of living and economic and social progress in the less-developed countries is desirable not only in the interests of those countries but also in the interests of the international community as a whole;

That achievement of these objectives would be facilitated by an increase in the international flow of capital, public and private, to assist in the development of the resources of the less-developed countries.'

Article 1

'The purposes of the Association are to promote economic development, increase productivity and thus raise standards of living in the less-developed areas of the world included within the Association's membership, in particular by providing finance to meet their important developmental requirements on terms which are more flexible and bear less heavily on the balance of payments than those of conventional loans, thereby furthering the developmental objectives of the International Bank for Reconstruction and Development (hereinafter called 'the Bank') and supplementing its activities.'

C. International Trade Organization

Article 1

' ... pledge themselves, individually and collectively, to promote national and international action designed to attain the following objectives:

1) To assure a large and steadily growing volume of real income and effective demand, to increase the production, consumption and exchange of goods, and thus to contribute a balanced and expanding world economy.

2) To foster and assist industrial and general economic development, particularly of those countries which are still in the early stages of industrial development, and to encourage the international flow of capital for productive investment.

3) To further the enjoyment by all countries, on equal terms, of access to the markets, products and productive facilities which are needed for their economic prosperity and development.

4) To promote on a reciprocal and mutually advantageous basis the reduction of tariffs and other barriers to trade and the elimination of discriminatory treatment to international commerce.

5) To enable countries, by increasing the opportunities for their trade and economic development, to abstain from measures which would disrupt world commerce, reduce productive employment or retard economic progress.

6) To facilitate through the promotion of mutual understanding, consultation and co-operation, the solution of problems relating to international trade in the fields of employment, economic development, commercial policy, business practices and commodity policy.'

D. The General Agreement on Tariffs and Trade

Preamble

' ... Recognising that their relations in the field of trade and economic endeavour should be conducted with a view to raising standards of living, ensuring full employment and a large and steadily growing volume of real income and effective demand, developing the full use of the resources of the world and expanding the production and exchange of goods,

Being desirous of contributing to these objectives by entering into reciprocal and mutually advantageous arrangements directed to the substantial reduction of tariffs and other barriers to trade and to the elimination of discriminatory treatment in international commerce ...'

E. United Nations Conference on Trade and Development

The United Nations General Assembly Resolution 1995 (XIX)

The principal functions of the Conference shall be:

'(a) To promote international trade, especially with a view to accelerating economic development, particularly trade between countries at different stages of development, between developing countries and between countries with different systems of economic and social organisation, taking into account the functions performed by existing international organisations;

(b) To formulate principles and policies on international trade and related problems of economic development;

(c) To make proposals for putting the said principles and policies into effect and to take such other steps within its competence as may be relevant to this end, having regard to differences in economic systems and stages of development;

(d) Generally, to review and facilitate the co-ordination of activities of other institutions within the United Nations system in the field of international trade and related problems of economic development, and in this regard to co-operate with the General Assembly and the Economic and Social Council with respect to the performance of their responsibilities for co-ordination under the Charter of the United Nations;

(e) To initiate action, where appropriate, in co-operation with the competent organs of the United Nations for the negotiation and adoption of multilateral legal instruments in the field of trade, with due regard to the adequacy of existing organs of negotiation and without duplication of their activities;

(f) To be available as a centre for harmonising the trade and related development policies of Governments and regional economic groupings in pursuance of Article 1 of the Charter;

(g) To deal with any other matters within the scope of its competence.'

Appendix II

List of Abbreviations

BIS	Bank for International Settlements
C-20	Committee of Twenty - the Committee of the Board of Governors of the IMF on Reform of the International Monetary System and Related Issues
CFF	Compensatory Financing Facility
DAC	Development Assistance Committee
EFF	Extended Fund Facility
EMS	European Monetary System
FAO	Food and Agriculture Organization
FPDI	Foreign private direct investment
FRNs	Floating rate notes
G5	Group of Five Countries (see Appendix III for country membership)
G10	Group of Ten Countries (see Appendix III for country membership)
GAB	General Arrangements to Borrow
GATT	General Agreement on Tariffs and Trade
GDP	Gross domestic product
GNP	Gross national product
GSP	Generalised System of Preferences
IBRD	International Bank for Reconstruction and Development
ICAs	International commodity agreements
ICSID	International Centre for the Settlement of Investment Disputes
IDA	International Development Association
IFAD	International Fund for Agricultural Development
IFC	International Finance Corporation
IGA	International Grains Arrangement

IIF	Institute of International Finance
IMF	International Monetary Fund
IPC	Integrated Programme for Commodities
ITO	International Trade Organization
lolr	Lender of last resort
MDBs	Multilateral Development Banks
MFA	Multifibre Arrangement
mfn	Most favoured nation
NICs	Newly industrialising countries
ODA	Official development assistance
OECD	Organization for Economic Co-operation and Development
OPEC	Organization of Petroleum Exporting Countries
SAL	Structural adjustment lending/loan
SDRs	Special Drawing Rights
Stabex	System to guarantee the stabilisation of earnings from ACP States' exports to the EEC of selected products on which the ACP economies depend
TNCs	Transnational Corporations
UNCTAD	United Nations Conference on Trade and Development
UNCTC	United Nations Centre on Transnational Corporations
UNDP	United Nations Development Programme
VERs	'Voluntary' export restraints

Appendix III

Note on Country Groupings

Countries have been grouped into various categories by the different international agencies. Where a country grouping has a precise coverage it is provided below. Some of the groupings differ only slightly in meaning or in country coverage, e.g. 'non-oil developing countries' (used by the IMF and the World Bank) and 'non-oil exporting developing countries' (used by the United Nations). In this Report, country groupings are not in every case used in a precise sense except where the terms have been used for statistical purposes.

UN and UNCTAD Definitions

1. Least-developed countries: three basic criteria for this category were adopted by the UN in the mid-1960s: per capita GDP of $100 or less, a share of manufacturing of 10 per cent or less of GDP, and a population with 20 per cent or less of literate persons aged 15 years or more. The following 36 countries are at present recognised as such: Afghanistan, Bangladesh, Benin, Bhutan, Botswana, Burundi, Cape Verde, Central African Republic, Chad, Comoros, Djibouti, Equatorial Guinea, Ethiopia, The Gambia, Guinea, Guinea-Bissau, Haiti, Laos, Lesotho, Malawi, Maldives, Mali, Nepal, Niger, Rwanda, Sao Tome and Principe, Sierra Leone, Somalia, Sudan, Tanzania, Togo, Uganda, Upper Volta, Yemen Arab Republic, Yemen Democratic Republic and Western Samoa.

2. The Socialist countries of Eastern Europe (referred to in the Report as East European countries) comprise Albania, Bulgaria, Czechoslovakia, German Democratic Republic, Hungary, Poland, Romania and the Soviet Union. A wider category of *centrally planned economy* countries would also include China, Kampuchea, Laos, Mongolia, North Korea and Vietnam.

3. Non-oil exporting developing countries: all countries except OECD members, OPEC members, the Socialist countries of Eastern Europe (as defined at 2 above), China, Israel and South Africa.

4. Oil-importing developing countries: non-oil exporting developing countries as defined at 3 above, except Bolivia, Egypt, Malaysia, Mexico, Peru, Syria, Tunisia and Zaire.

IMF and World Bank Definitions

5. Low-income developing countries: all countries whose 1981 per capita income was less than $410.

6. Middle-income developing countries: those developing countries with 1981 per capita income of $410 and above.

7. Oil-exporting countries: those countries whose oil exports (net of any crude oil imports) both accounted for at least two-thirds of the country's total exports and were at least 100 million barrels a year during 1978-80. A similar, but not identical group to OPEC: Algeria, Indonesia, Iran, Iraq, Kuwait, Libya, Nigeria, Oman, Qatar, Saudi Arabia, United Arab Emirates and Venezuela.

8. Non-oil developing countries: all developing countries except those listed at 7 above.

9. Industrial countries: all OECD members (see 13 below) except Greece, Portugal and Turkey which are regarded as 'middle-income' developing countries. The term industrialised countries as used in this Report refers to all OECD members.

OECD Definitions

10. Newly industrialising countries: this category is variously defined but includes countries at a relatively advanced level of economic development with a substantial and dynamic industrial sector and with close links to the international trade, finance and investment system. The OECD category of newly industrialised countries comprises Argentina, Brazil, Greece, Hong Kong, Republic of Korea, Mexico, Portugal, Singapore, Spain, Taiwan and Yugoslavia.

11. Non-OPEC developing countries: all countries except OECD members (other than Greece, Portugal, Spain and Turkey), OPEC members (other than Indonesia and Nigeria), the Socialist countries of Eastern Europe, Mongolia, North Korea and South Africa.

General: Other Groups with Defined Membership

12. OPEC: Organization of Petroleum Exporting Countries comprises Algeria, Ecuador, Gabon, Indonesia, Iran, Iraq, Kuwait, Libya, Nigeria, Qatar, Saudi Arabia, United Arab Emirates and Venezuela. The Development Assistance Committee (DAC) of the OECD defines 'OPEC countries' as excluding Indonesia and Nigeria which it regards as 'low-income' and 'middle-income' respectively (see 5 and 6 above for definition).

13. OECD: Organization for Economic Co-operation and Development comprises Australia, Austria, Belgium, Canada, Denmark, Finland, France, Federal Republic of Germany, Greece, Iceland, Ireland, Italy, Japan, Luxembourg, Netherlands, New Zealand, Norway, Portugal, Spain, Sweden, Switzerland, Turkey, United Kingdom and United States.

14. Group of Ten (G10): Belgium, Canada, France, Federal Republic of Germany, Italy, Japan, Netherlands, Sweden, United Kingdom and United States.

15. Group of Five (G5): France, Federal Republic of Germany, Japan, United Kingdom and United States.

16. Intergovernmental Group of Twenty-four on International Monetary Affairs (G24): comprises eight developing countries from each of Africa, Asia, and Central and South America. The countries are as follows: Algeria, Egypt, Ethiopia, Gabon, Ghana, Ivory Coast, Nigeria, Zaire; India, Iran, Lebanon, Pakistan, Philippines, Sri Lanka, Syria, Yugoslavia; Argentina, Brazil, Colombia, Guatemala, Mexico, Peru, Trinidad and Tobago, Venezuela.

Appendix IV

Members of the Study Group

Professor Gerald K. Helleiner
(Chairman)

Professor, Department of
Economics, University of
Toronto; Vice-Chairman,
North-South Institute, Ottawa

Professor Conrad Blyth

Professor of Economics and
Head of Economics
Department, University of
Auckland; Deputy Chairman,
New Zealand Planning Council

H.E. Mr. Kenneth Dadzie

High Commissioner of Ghana
to the United Kingdom;
formerly Director-General for
Development and International
Economic Co-operation, United
Nations

Mr. William Demas

President, Caribbean
Development Bank; Chairman,
UN Committee for
Development Planning;
formerly Secretary-General,
Caribbean Community

Professor Stuart Harris	Director and Professor of Resource Economics, Centre for Resources and Environmental Studies, Australian National University, Canberra; formerly Deputy Secretary, Department of Overseas Trade, Australia
H.E. Dr. Lal Jayawardena	Ambassador, Ministry of Foreign Affairs, Colombo; formerly Ambassador of Sri Lanka to Belgium, the Netherlands and Luxembourg and to the European Communities, and Secretary to the Treasury and to the Ministry of Finance, Sri Lanka
Sir Jeremy Morse	Chairman, Lloyds Bank Plc; formerly Chairman of the Deputies of the Committee of the Board of Governors of the IMF on Reform of the International Monetary System and Related Issues (the Committee of Twenty)
Mr. Harry M. Osha	Executive Chairman, Milestone Investment Services Ltd; formerly Managing Director, Nigerian Industrial Development Bank Ltd. and Deputy Permanent Secretary, Federal Ministry of Finance, Nigeria
Dr. I.G. Patel	Director, Indian Institute of Management, Ahmedabad, India; formerly Governor of the Reserve Bank of India, Deputy Administrator UNDP, and Secretary to the Ministry of Finance, India

Secretariat

(Economic Affairs Division, Commonwealth Secretariat)

Dr. B. Persaud — Director and Secretary of Study Group

Mr. Q.S. Siddiqi — Assistant Director

Mr. I.R. Thomas — Assistant Director

Mr. D.I. Huntley — Chief Officer (Economics)

Dr. S.K. Rao — Chief Officer (Economics)

Mr. D.L. Dodhia — Senior Economics Officer

Miss E.R. Minto — Senior Economics Officer

Printed by The Chameleon Press Limited, 5–25 Burr Road, London SW18 4SG, England.